THE INTERNET OF INTELLIGENT THINGS

Your Guide to The Connected Future

Dave Evans

Copyright © 2020 Dave Evans

All rights reserved

Material referenced or cited is protected via respective copyrights as applicable.

No part of this book may be reproduced, or stored in a retrieval system, or transmitted in any form or by any means, electronic, mechanical, photocopying, recording, or otherwise, without express written permission of the author.

ISBN: 978-1-7351091-1-4

To Sunny, Kyle, and Max. My most precious things.

With a special thank you to Jonathan Nash, my long-lost brother, for his inspiration to write this book.

CONTENTS

Title Page
Copyright
Dedication

1. Welcome to the Future	1
2. The History of the Internet. A Look Back, Before We Look Forward.	10
3. The Cloud	22
4. The History of the Internet of Things	27
5. The Internet of Everything	32
6. It's the Connections That Matter	34
7. Security and Privacy	39
8. Blockchain	48
9. Power in Numbers	57
10. How IoT Will Change Everything	60
11. The Zettaflood Is Coming	64
12. The Dark Side of Big Data	69
13. Understanding AI	77
14. The Current State of AI	91
15. Intelligence for Sale	99
16. Rise of the Machines	103
17. A Quantum Leap	108
18. Human 2.0	113
19. Exponential Opportunities	122
20. Not Above the Law	126
21. Intelligent Things Enable Intelligent Solutions.	141

22. Final Thoughts	148
Author's Note	150
Appendix – Predicting the Future	151
Acknowledgment and Attribution	155
References	156

1. WELCOME TO THE FUTURE

"Behind me is infinite power. Before me is endless possibility. Around me is boundless opportunity. Why should I fear?"
- Stella Stuart, Author

You may think you already live in a connected, intelligent world. Smartphones ensure many of us have a powerful computer with Internet access on hand at all times. Technologies like self-driving cars, smart homes, and virtual assistants have capabilities that not so long ago might have seemed like science fiction. There are so many Internet-connected devices - many of them everyday objects like household appliances - that terms like "Internet of Things" and "Internet of Everything" have come into widespread use. It's easy to look at the technological marvels of the modern world and conclude, "The future is now."

But the truth is, "the future" has barely even *begun*, and it is coming far faster than you might think. Technologies already in development and social trends already well underway are pushing us rapidly and inexorably into a world that will be exponentially more intelligent and more connected. Not just an Internet of Things, but an Internet of *Intelligent* Things.

This book is your guide to that coming future.

I've spent decades as a professional futurist. My expert analysis of technological and social trends has been sought by some of the world's most successful companies and executives, including a decade as the chief futurist of Cisco during my 24-year tenure there. I've spoken to Fortune 100 CEOs and crowds of tens of thousands. But right now, I'm talking to you because the future isn't just going to impact major corporations. It's going to affect all of us.

Don't believe me? Let me introduce you to a friend of mine. Her name is Sally.

Sally is a normal person, just like you, but with two important differences. The first difference is that Sally is a fictional character in a thought experiment. The second is that she lives in 2038. But if we spend just one day with Sally, we'll see how even an ordinary day in the life of an average person will be completely and totally transformed by the Internet of Intelligent Things.

A Day in the Life

Sally is awoken by her digital assistant. She has chosen to call her assistant Rosie, inspired by her love of the 1960's animated sitcom The Jetsons.[i] She watched re-runs of the Jetsons as a child and has fond memories of the show, and in particular the female humanoid robot that is her assistant's namesake. It doesn't really matter what she calls her assistant, as it recognizes her voice thanks to advanced biometrics. A name simply serves to humanize the technology. It's more for Sally's sake than Rosie's.

Rosie is not a physical device on her bedside table, but rather a service integrated into her life. Microphones incorporated into lighting fixtures around her home pick up every sound. Privacy is no longer a concern thanks to global legislation mandating end-user control of personal data. The penalties for non-compliance are so steep that companies make their money on services instead of mining and selling users' data.

The lights in Sally's home are coordinated with the sunrise, so the lights gradually turn on while they also change their hue.

Her connected mattress informs Rosie that Sally had a good night's sleep. Rosie relays that information to Sally along with some other pertinent information about the day such as the weather, and her schedule.

Sally showers and brushes her teeth. Her toothbrush notices a small cavity and instructs Rosie to schedule a dentist appointment next week. Rosie complies and mentions it to Sally. Not the greatest thing Sally wants to hear first thing in the morning, but necessary. With all this technology and advancement, "Why do we still get cavities?" Sally ponders.

Rosie suggests a coordinated outfit for the day and Sally gets dressed.

As she walks into the kitchen, she is greeted by her husband and her twin children. Her husband woke an hour earlier to help get the children ready for school. The children are practicing for a biology test later today. They have both donned augmented reality glasses and are collaborating together while exploring the organelles within a cell. They use their hands and voice to manipulate the 3D visualizations displayed in space in front of them and are quizzed by Rosie on the many types of organelles in a cell. Sensors inside the glasses rest on the temples of the head and pick up subtle readings via neural sensors. Coupled with eye-tracking attention technology, the glasses ensure that the children are paying attention and not gaming the system. If their attention strays, the software on the glasses automatically adjusts to compensate, speeding up, slowing down, or changing topics as needed. There is a reason these are called smart glasses!

The incentive for paying attention and doing their homework is a reward of more time on the gaming service. In addition to the gaming service, the glasses notify their teacher that the children have done their homework. Monotonous, rote, tedious homework is a thing of the past. Today's homework is immersive, engaging, and fun.

Sally forgoes breakfast today. Coffee for Sally this morning is black. She usually prefers it with cream and a little sugar, but Rosie knows that Sally has a blood test today and cannot eat until after the test. The test is routine, but her wearable has noticed that she has been low on iron so asked Rosie to schedule a doctor's appointment.

Sally and her husband gather the kids and head to work. Both have office jobs that they enjoy. Sally doesn't always have to go into the office, she has more than enough technological capability at home, but she enjoys getting away, compartmentalizing work and home. She needs to work late tonight so her husband will pick up the kids. He'll instruct the car to pick her up later.

As the family leaves for work, the home goes into frugal mode. It intelligently adjusts its energy usage. The thermostat turns down, the lights turn off, and the appliances check with the utility company on energy pricing, so they know when to operate. Although their home runs on green energy, it is still purchased from the energy company who can generate it at scale.

Outside, the robotic lawnmower quietly springs to life. It notifies the irrigation system to delay its start time so it can mow the lawn. Sensors in the lawn notify the lawnmower that it is low on nitrogen. The lawnmower adds that to its routine and will deposit some fertilizer from its hopper as it mows.

The house secures itself. The doors and windows lock. They don't need to set an alarm, as the home knows when they are away and automatically switches to sentry mode. There are no door or window sensors, no motion sensors. Instead, disruptions in the wireless signals in the home can inform Rosie if there are intruders or anomalies.

The coffee machine notifies Rosie that they are low on coffee and Rosie adds it to the shopping list. A drone delivery is expected later that day and it should arrive then.

Sally and her husband chat and share a few jokes with the kids as the car drives them to school and then work. They all sit facing one another as autonomous cars do not have the same seating constraints as the older "manual" models. A passenger can swivel around if needed to take control of the car, but that hasn't been needed for years.

As the vehicle approaches an intersection, the car informs the vestigial traffic light that it is approaching. As no other cars are coming in the opposite direction it quickly changes so that Sally's car can turn left.

The car stops at the school and the children hop out. Rosie, who is also integrated into the vehicle, reminds the children to grab their backpacks that they have left in the car. Sally and her husband drive off. Sally drops off her husband, kisses him goodbye, and proceeds to her office.

Is this new hyper-connected world, Sally could just as easily work from home. Very few jobs are tied to a physical location. However, in the early 2020's studies showed that a blurring of the work and home life caused an increase in stress and had a dramatic effect on life expectancy. As a result, a growing movement of separating work from home life arose. It was no longer a badge of honor of how many hours you worked; in fact, it was frowned upon. Although life expectancy was now well past one hundred, life was still too short to work all the time. Some saw this coming decades earlier. In 2017 France for example, a new labor law gave employees the "right to disconnect" from email, smartphones and other electronic leashes once their working day has ended.[ii] This would mark the beginning of a global shift in work perspective.

Work-life balance beliefs aside, Sally also simply liked getting out of the house to go to work. This logical separation allowed her to focus on her job when in the office and her family when she was home, without the distractions of each other.

Upon arriving at her office, she grabs her things and the vehicle drives away. Her car will spend the next few hours in a rideshare service where it will pick up and drop off people who have requested a vehicle. This pays for the cost of the vehicle and minimizes the number of vehicles that need to be on the roads.

Sally enters her office as it comes alive. The glass windows become transparent, the lights turn on, the temperature reaches its ideal state (the car already notified the office Sally was on her way), and soft, ambient music plays in the background. The days of open office concepts have come and gone. Studies have shown that they are not as effective as once believed. There is plenty of open spaces in the office should a group need to get together.

Sally spends the next hour catching on work and preparing for her day. Rosie interrupts, reminding her that she has a video conference call with some clients in Japan. Moments later, Akiri-san, her client in Akita, Japan appears on screen.

"Ohayo gozaimasu" she says to him respectfully.

Immediately the English translation is displayed on her screen. Ohayo gozaimasu is a formal Japanese greeting and is preferred over a more casual greeting when making acquaintance.

Although the computer is more than capable of translating her English perfectly, it has become tradition to begin the conversation with an authentic greeting first. This demonstrates respect and is generally considered appropriate protocol.

As they converse, Akiri-san speaks in Japanese and his words are immediately displayed on Sally's screen in English. On Akiri-san's screen, Sally's English is automatically transcribed to the appropriate kanji, hiragana, or katakana (the modern Japanese writing system) for Akiri-san. In addition to the written word, Sally hears Akiri-san in flawless English, with the same tone and accent. Akiri in turn hears Sally speak perfect Japanese. Although they both speak their natural languages, cloud-based translation services automatically detect and translate in real-time.

As they continue to chat, keywords such as people's names, places, and things are automatically picked out of the conversation and the computer screen shows relevant articles, web pages, and images.

They conclude the conversation and mention that they look forward to chatting again next month. Rosie picks up this cue in the conversation and adds the meeting to both of their calendars. Sally bids Akiri-san, "Sayonara", the standard "Bye" or "Goodbye" in Japanese.

Rosie reminds Sally that she has a doctor's appointment and lets Sally know that a car is waiting for her.

Sally drops by the doctor's office and has her blood drawn by a "hemobot"; a common practice for doctors' offices in 2038. Hemobots are fast, efficient, and find the vein every time thanks to an onboard near-infrared scanner. Within minutes she gets her results, indicating that she is indeed low in iron as she suspected, thanks to her wearable. Some simple dietary changes are recommended to resolve the low blood iron. By now she is famished having only had a small cup of black coffee all day, so she decides to grab a bite of food on her way back to the office.

She stops by a local restaurant and considers ordering some steak. It's high in iron, and just what the doctor ordered, she thinks to herself. She orders a lab-grown steak, standard fare in dining. By 2038 most proteins are grown artificially in huge clean rooms. Lab-grown is still the moniker used to differentiate them from their natural counterparts, but they have quickly become mainstream as sensitivity towards sustainability becomes a global trend. Gone are the fears of lab-grown proteins. These proteins are imperceptible from the "real thing", are chemical-free, have the perfect amount of fat, and are cheaper as they can be produced with much less land, water, and food.

She asks for her steak sliced and placed on a salad. A few minutes later her lunch arrives, and she presses her fork into a piece of meat, anticipating the first bite. Immediately her personal computer buzzes, warning her. Microscopic sensors on the fork had picked up traces of pine nuts in the dish. A nut she is severely allergic to. The fork notified her computer in milliseconds and averted a severe reaction.

She exchanges her dish for a similar one without incident. She gets up and walk out. There's no need to request a check as the cost of her food has been automatically paid by Rosie. Rosie had picked up the conversation she had earlier with her server and knows exactly what she had ordered. Rosie queried the restaurants' systems to determine the lunch costs, and even added on a small gratuity.

The rest of Sally's workday is uneventful. She has decided to work late to get a jump on a few projects so she can leave early at the end of the week for a wedding.

As it gets later, she gets a notification from Rosie that the children have arrived home from school with her husband. She settles in for a couple more hours of work. As her colleagues leave, their offices shut down and their lights dim. They do not shut off completely as the building knows she is still there. It gets a little chilly so the building heats just her section. It knows not to needlessly heat sections of the floor where there is no one. This reduces the buildings energy costs significantly.

She wraps up her work and heads out of the building. Her car is waiting for her. As she gets into her car, she notices a chill in the air, and some light rain. She's not the only one to notice. The traffic lights notice too. They automatically adjust their changing frequency to force traffic to slow down a little to reduce accidents. The traffic lights are more wireless beacons than they are visible alerts. They wirelessly communicate to vehicles as well as to one another. The changing of the lights remains for the very few legacy cars still on the road. In a few more years, they will no longer be needed and will go the way of the payphone.

The building notices she has left for the day and ensures all doors and windows are closed before it hibernates for the night.

It's getting late and there are few cars on the road. As her car takes her home, streetlights illuminate and extinguish automatically as she drives past them. The car doesn't need them as it can see perfectly fine in total darkness, but they remain on for her comfort.

The car slows down. Sally looks out of the window to notice an ambulance speeding by. The ambulance notified all vehicles in the area that it was coming, and they responded accordingly.

Her vehicle notifies her that it is low on energy and that it must stop for a quick re-charge. The vehicle pulls into a charging station and in a matter of seconds is re-charged. Batteries have given way to sodium-based super capacitors that can re-charge in seconds without Sally needing to do anything. The vehicle slips over an inductive charging plate and in quickly re-charged. In similar fashion to the restaurant, the fees are paid automatically. The inductive charger and vehicle agree on the amount of energy used and the fees are deducted from her account.

Sally arrives home and her home welcomes her. Lights illuminate the walkway, and the front door unlocks. She is greeted by her husband and goes in to say goodnight to her children. They are excited to see her and share good news about their biology test.

The vehicle will not be needed for the rest of the night, so it too goes into sentry mode. It will be an extra set of "eyes" and "ears' for the house while the family sleeps.

In the course of her day, Sally interacted with more than 20,000 connected devices. Most were invisible to her. These were unlike the devices of 2018. These devices adapted to changing scenarios. They had a close relationship to her and made her day better. They didn't beep at her every five minutes. They didn't require jumping from application to application to interact with. They just worked, and they worked flawlessly.

She didn't work for the technology. The technology was finally intelligent enough to work for her.

The Internet of Intelligent Things

Sally's life may sound far removed from your own, but this is not some pie-in-the-sky utopian dream. Many factors are now in play that will make this future not just a possibility, but an inevitability. As you read this, billions of dollars are being invested into artificial intelligence companies and solutions.[iii] The number of objects with Internet connections is increasing at a staggering rate, and the Internet connections themselves are becoming much faster. We are producing data at an unprecedented rate that dwarfs all of human history, and to keep up storage is becoming more efficient and migrating to the cloud.

Individually, each of these technologies and trends are changing how we shop, how we communicate, how we manufacture goods, how we grow our food, how we manage our homes, and ultimately how we live our lives. As transformative as they are, however, something much bigger, something that encapsulates all of these trends, is on the horizon—The Internet of Intelligent Things.

The devices that Sally interacted within our fictional day in the life were not "dumb" connected devices, they were "intelligent" connected devices. The Internet of Things had merged with artificial intelligence.

As advancements in hardware and artificial intelligence make it easier and more effective to add intelligence to connected devices, connectivity will become ubiquitous, seamless, and affordable—rather than noticing that something is connected, you will notice when something isn't connected. Connectivity of everything will simply be an expectation, as it was for Sally. And each of those connected devices will not only use their own artificial intelligence to make better decisions, they will be connected to *each other*, creating a powerful global intelligence.

This book explores this coming era, from the background and history that brought us to this point, to the technologies driving this transformation, to the implications it will have for humanity and the opportunities it will provide. While this book touches on many of the technical aspects of these technologies, it has been written to be approachable and does not presuppose a deep technical background on behalf of the reader.

The primary purpose of the book is to bring awareness to some of the technological forces that will shape our future, and give you, the reader, the background to understand these trends in more detail. Whether or not you agree with every specific prognostication, you should be aware of the changes coming.

I am often asked where I get all of my information, which books to read, what websites to visit, what's next, etc. The reality is that there are vast amounts of information on all of these topics, yet some are daunting to consume. Facts are often mixed with hype and getting a clear, succinct explanation of these topics in plain language is often illusive.

I decided to write a book that anyone could pick up, with little to no background in technology, computer science, or engineering, and understand the technologies that are shaping our future. Devoid of unnecessary jargon, with clear explanations and examples, this book will give you a basic foundation of how the Internet of Things is evolving into something much bigger. It will provide you with an understanding of the Internet of Things, machine learning, big data, the forces that are shaping these technologies, and how all of these trends will converge to create the Internet of Intelligent Things. For those who want to dig deeper into any of these topics, I've provided an extensive list of references, and have made a good faith effort to point readers in the direction of helpful sources on many of the more complex subjects in this book.

No matter your background or profession, there is no escaping the technologies that are shaping our lives. Having a basic understanding will help you make better decisions professionally and personally. If you're looking for a book you can read in an afternoon or two, that will give you an overall understanding of these technologies and a glimpse of what is to come, then look no further. This book is for you.

The future is bringing us along for a wild ride. I hope you enjoy the book.

2. THE HISTORY OF THE INTERNET. A LOOK BACK, BEFORE WE LOOK FORWARD.

"Big things have small beginnings."
- The android David in *Prometheus* (spoken, as an homage to *Lawrence of Arabia*).

A good futurist understands that predicting the future is impossible without an understanding of the past. Observing a historical trend can yield critical insight into where it might eventually lead, and only by understanding the origins of a technology can one make any sort of educated estimate about how it might develop going forward. So, to understand how and why we will soon have an Internet of Intelligent Things, we must first understand how we came to have an Internet in the first place.

Few things have shaped our world like the Internet has. As of this writing, more than 4.57 billion people were active Internet users, and usage is growing rapidly.[iv] Between 2000 and 2015, Internet users increased almost seven-fold from 6.5% to 43% of the global population.[v]

A quote from the 1998 U.S. Department report The Emerging Digital Economy illustrates how rapidly the Internet has been adopted:

"The Internet's pace of adoption eclipses all other technologies that preceded it. Radio was in existence 38 years before 50 million people tuned in; TV took 13 years to reach that benchmark. Sixteen years after the first PC kit came out, 50 million people were using one. Once it was opened to the general public, the Internet crossed that line in four years."[vi]

Today, billions of devices connect to the Internet with estimates in the

20 to 30 billion range.[vii]

It's hard to imagine a world without the Internet. It is the foundation of the World Wide Web, email, instant messaging, and many more technologies that have become ubiquitous in modern society. From paying bills, to shopping, to planning travel, to staying in touch, the Internet has become indispensable.

Yet the Internet had a humble beginning.

The 1960's were a defining time in American history. Rock and roll was in full swing, the Vietnam war was being waged, the country was devastated by the assassinations of John F. Kennedy and Martin Luther King Jr., the world was on the edge of their seat watching the Cuban Missile Crisis, the civil rights movement re-shaped America, the baby boom was well underway, and Neil Armstrong became the first human to step on the Moon.

But quietly, during this tumultuous time, the foundational elements of a technology that would forever shape our lives were being created.

The history of the Internet can be dated to the early 1960's. In August of 1962, J.C.R. Licklider of MIT crafted a series of memos discussing his "Galactic Network" concept. This concept described "social interactions that could be enabled through networking."[viii] Licklider envisioned "a globally interconnected set of computers through which everyone could quickly access data and programs from any location[ix]." The concept was very similar to the Internet of today.

In October of 1962, Licklider became the first head of the computer research program at DARPA (Defense Advanced Research Projects Agency).[x] While he was at DARPA, he convinced his colleagues of the importance of this networking concept.[xi]

In 1969, DARPA took the project further by interconnecting four university computers. These university computers became the very first hosts on the ARPANET.[xii] The Internet as it would later be called, was born, but it still had a lot of growing up to do. This modest beginning would ultimately become the foundation for today's massive, globally-interconnected Internet.

Although initially developed by the U.S. military, Charles M. Herzfeld, the former director of ARPA, stated that the ARPANET was not created due to military needs and that it "came out of our frustration that there were only a limited number of large, powerful research computers in the country and that many research investigators who should have access were geographically separated from them."[xiii]

Initially, the ARPANET consisted of four IMPs (Interface Message Processors).[xiv] An IMP was a node[xv] (communications equipment) used to interconnect participating networks to the ARPANET. IMPs were the first generation of gateways, which are similar to today's network routers. A router is a networking device that *routes* (or forwards) network information from one part of the network to another. If you connect to the Internet from your home or office, there is a likely a router that connects your home or office network to the rest of the Internet. Today's routers are many times faster than the original IMPs, but their core function is the same.

IMPs were used from the late 1960s to, remarkably, as recently as 1989. Each IMP was located in the respective research labs of UCLA (University of California, Los Angeles), Stanford Research Institute, University of California, Santa Barbara and the University of Utah.

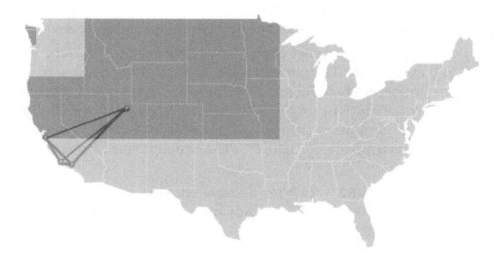

Figure 1 – THE ARPANET, DECEMBER 5, 1969

In 1969, there were only four computers connected when the ARPANET was created. By 1981 there were 213 hosts, adding approximately 100 new hosts every 5 years. As we'll soon see, that growth is dwarfed by the rate at which we are adding devices today. It's quite likely that you have more connected devices in your home than the entire ARPANET had in 1969!

The first exchange of data over this new network occurred between computers at UCLA and the Stanford Research Institute.

On October 29th, 1969, at 10:30PM, UCLA student Charley Kline types the letter "l" onto a computer terminal. He immediately follows it with the letter "o." Moments later the remote system at Stanford that he is attempting to communicate to, crashes.

This brief message, "lo", was the first message ever transmitted on the ARPANET. About an hour or so later, the system was restored, and the word "login" was successfully transmitted. Amusingly, the same three letters that are used to imply laughing out loud (LOL) in today's text messages and email appear to be the first three letters transmitted across the Internet.

ARPARNET's initial purpose was to primarily enable scientific and academic users to communicate and share information with one another, but that was just the beginning.

One of the breakthroughs of the ARPANET, compared to earlier forms of communication, was that it took advantage of a new concept known as packet switching. These *packets* of data could be routed, using different paths, and reconstructed at their final destination.

Computer World explains the difference between circuit switch and packet-switched networks[xvi]: "Prior to packet switched networks, circuit-switched networks dominated communications. Designed in 1878, circuit-switched networks reserve a dedicated channel for the entire communication. In modern circuit-switched networks, electronic signals pass through several switches before a connection is established. And during a call, no other network traffic can use those switches."

You may recall images of the old telephone switchboards in movies.[xvii] Operators would sit at these switchboards and physically plug-in wires to create circuits between telephones on the network. When that circuit was in use, no one else could use that line. This is an early example of a circuit switched network.

While fine for the early days of telephony, this type of approach is clearly inefficient for building scalable, global networks.

"In packet-based networks, however, the message gets broken into small data packets that seek out the most efficient route as circuits become available."[xviii]

As an analogy for how packet-switched networks operate, it is useful to think about how the post office works. When you write a letter to someone, you place the letter in an envelope, and write the address of the recipient on the front of the envelope. You may also include your own address on the envelope too. This tells the post office where to send (or route) the letter, as well as where it came from.

Now let's say that you had an extremely long letter that did not fit in a single envelope. You might number each page of your letter, then break up that letter into separate pages, and send that letter in multiple envelopes. Then, when the recipient gets your letter, they can simply assemble the entire letter in the correct order.

This is similar in concept to how packet-switched networks work. They take your message, perhaps an email, or a photo you're posting on your favorite social media site and break it down into smaller packets. Each packet, along with a header, is sent to the destination. The header contains information such as who sent it, and where it is intended for.

The diagram below illustrates the composition of an IP version 4 packet with a data payload. Unlike the envelope analogy, it has a few more fields of information. Of the 14 fields, 13 are required and 1 is optional. You can read more about the IPv4 packet structure if interested on Wikipedia.[xix]

Version	Header Length	Type of Service	Total Length
Identification		Flags	Fragment Offset
Time to Live	Upper Layer	Header Checksum	
Source IP Address			
Destination IP Address			
Options			
Data			

Figure 2 - IPV4 PACKET ILLUSTRATED

The networking devices called routers that I mentioned earlier, route these packets. They deconstruct the packet to understand how to route it. They may even modify the packet in transit in order to successfully route it. Once received by the recipient device, the messages are reassembled in the correct order. This is typically done in milliseconds and is imperceptible to the end-user.

Using the post office analogy, these routers perform a similar function to the postal van, transporting your mail.

Networks are similar to the roads on which we drive our cars. There is typically more than one way to get to a given destination. You might take an alternate route due to traffic congestion, and computer networks are no different.

Each individual packet may go a different route, depending on things such as network congestion. The destination device knows how to reassemble all the packets in the correct order. The packets pass through many networking devices en route to their destination, and the header tells each router how to send the message along. Among other details, the routers maintain routing tables.[xx] You can think of the routing table as the map you might reference when driving around town. Just like a map helps you navigate roadways to your destination; a routing table helps a router determine how to route your packets. This is an oversimplification, as routers are sophisticated, complex devices that do much more, but the core principles remain.

Packet switching is the primary basis for data communications in computer networks worldwide today.[xxi]

Although packet switching helped solve the message delivery challenge, for networks to function reliably and consistently they would still require a set of rules and guidelines known as *protocols*.[xxii] In the networking world, "network protocols are formal standards and policies comprised of rules, procedures and formats that define communication between two or more devices over a network."[xxiii]

In the early days of the Internet, companies developed their own protocols for how networks should communicate.

In 1975 Digital Equipment Corporation developed a suite of networking protocols known as DECnet.[xxiv] Originally designed to connect to PDP-11 minicomputers[xxv], it later evolved into one of the first peer-to-peer networking architectures.[xxvi]

In 1984 IBM developed a protocol called Token Ring.[xxvii] This was a local area network (LAN) protocol. Unlike the Internet that spans the globe, a LAN is a small, localized network. It may be as small as a few devices connected in a single room, or as large as a few buildings connected together.

Your home network is a LAN and is part of the broader Internet.

In the Token Ring model, a node on the LAN could only transmit when it was in possession of a token. A token was a sequence of bits (we'll get to those later) that was passed to each node in turn. This worked well for small networks but was arguably not a scalable model.

In 1985, Apple released AppleTalk.[xxviii] This was the primary protocol used by Apple devices throughout the 1980s and 1990s. It was in fact a suite of protocols, proprietary to Apple. As is often the case with Apple, it was relatively user-friendly and did not require much to set it up. It also did not require any sort of centralized router or server.

These are just a few examples, and there were many more. In these early days of the Internet many companies were developing their own protocols. While initially, this may not seem like an issue, as most networks were local area networks, meaning that these were networks inside of a building, that did not need to talk to other networks. But as the Internet would evolve from local area networks to wide area networks, connecting buildings, cities, and countries to each other, this was going to be a problem. It would be like a cocktail party where each person speaks a different language—communication would be incredibly difficult. There needed to be a way to translate languages between one another.

For the Internet, this solution was known as the multi-protocol router.[xxix] IP, AppleTalk, DECNet, and Token Ring are examples of these protocols. A multi-protocol router is a bit like a translator at that cocktail party.

William (Bill) Yeager is credited with developing the first router while he was a staff researcher at Stanford university. Initially this router routed something known as PUP, or PARC universal packet for the Xerox PARC (Palo Alto Research Center) systems and mainframes. According to Bill, late in 1981 his boss came to him and said "IP is coming down the pipe. Figure out what you can do with it."[xxx] Bill put some IP router code in his router, and the multi-protocol router was born.

With so many protocols to choose from, why did TCP/IP become the dominant standard? History shows that it almost wasn't.

In 1974, the Institute of Electrical and Electronics Engineers (IEEE)[xxxi] published a paper entitled "A Protocol for Packet Network Intercommunication."[xxxii] This paper was authored by Vint Cerf[xxxiii] who, as we'll learn shortly, is widely regarded as the "father of the Internet", and Bob Kahn[xxxiv], an American electrical engineer. In this paper they describe "an internetworking protocol for sharing resources using packet switching among network nodes."[xxxv] This was to become the basis for TCP/IP, an informal moniker for the "Transmission Control Protocol and User Datagram Protocol at the transport layer and the Internet Protocol at the internet layer." TCP/IP would emerge to become the de facto standard that runs the global Internet.

Before TCP/IP, another standard known as OSI (Open Systems Interconnection[xxxvi]) seemed liked it would be the inevitable choice. At its height, in the mid-1980s, thousands of engineers and policymakers, globally, were working on standardizing OSI. However, just a few years later in the early 1990s, TCP/IP had taken a stronghold and OSI was left behind. Why was this? In short, it was a case of technology taking the path of least resistance. OSI was burdened with bureaucracy and TCP/IP was viewed as a more open, nimble solution. For a more complete history of why TCP/IP won over OSI, the IEEE Spectrum article: "OSI: The Internet That Wasn't. How TCP/IP eclipsed the Open Systems Interconnection standards to become the global protocol for computer networking"[xxxvii] is a worthwhile read.

This was a significant milestone in the history of the Internet, as it now meant that networks could talk to each other. Cisco Systems, where I first started in the networking industry in 1990, was one of the first companies to develop this technology. It is no surprise then that Cisco's first tagline was "The science of networking networks." In the early days, it was all about connecting disparate networks to one another. Without innovations like the multi-protocol router, there might not be a single Internet today, but rather many smaller, purpose-built ones.

This was an exciting time to be involved in the networking industry. Many of the barriers to interoperability had been removed, and the focus now was on innovation. Little did we know at the time how significant the Internet would become.

Today the Internet predominately utilizes a protocol called IP, or Internet Protocol.[xxxviii] If you've ever configured the networking settings on your computer, you've likely seen the IP address displayed as a 12-digit, period delimited number. This IP address is your computer's logical location on the Internet. Think of it as your computer's street address on a very long street called the Internet.

An IP address contains four numbers separated by periods. Each number can have a value from 0 to 255. This number contains information about the network, its sub-network and the host. Any device wishing to participate on the Internet needs a unique IP address. For example, as I'm writing this book the IP address of my computer is 76.21.2.144.

Why are the numbers separated by periods? The periods are arbitrary, it could have just as easily been dashes, or commas. They simply serve to delineate the four numbers. Without some sort of delineation, it would be difficult to break down an IP address. And you need to be able to break down an IP address in order to determine how to route the packets.

Each one of the four numbers in an IPv4 address is known as an 8-bit number. In computer science you can represent a number from 0-255 using 8 bits. As there are 4 of these numbers, there are a total of 32 bits (4 numbers x 8 bits per number).

Why bits? Well, computers as powerful as they are can only represent information in one of two states - a 0 or a 1. This is slowly changing however, with the emergence of a new type of computer known as a quantum computer. Quantum computers are in their infancy. I touch on them toward the end of this book. They will not replace traditional computers anytime soon, but if and when they do, computing is going to be fundamentally different.

Back to the zeros and ones. This is due to how computers are designed; more specifically the components they use. One of these core components is a transistor.[xxxix] These transistors, among other things, act as tiny switches. A switch can either be open or closed, on or off. As a result, these transistors can represent a state of 0 or 1. A 0 means the switch (transistor) is open, whereas a 1 means the switch (transistor) is closed. Two states may not seem much, but as we'll learn in the "Not above the law" chapter, a lowly bit can be incredibly powerful. Modern computers contain billions of transistors[xl] enabling them to manipulate billions of bits, billions of times a second.

When buying a computer, you may have heard the technician or salesperson talking about the speed of the computer. For example, the computer I'm using to write this book has a central processing unit (CPU) with a speed of 1.99 GHz. The CPU is the part of the computer than handles basic arithmetic and logic functions in addition to a few other important functions.[xli] In the 1.99 gigahertz speed example, giga means billion, and hertz refers to the cycles per second. Therefore, the CPU in my computer can be refreshed at almost 2 billion times per second. Said another way, 2 billion times a second, the billions of transistors in that CPU can be examined and updated. This is bit manipulation at an incredible scale. As we'll learn shortly, it gets even more impressive, as computer CPUs now have multiple "cores", each enabling them to manipulate billions of bits in parallel.

For now, back to IP addresses. Breaking down an IP address is important, as each set of numbers have meaning. Each 8-bit part is known as an *octet*.[xlii] So, in the example of my IP address, 76.21.2.144, 76 is an octet, as is 21, as is 2 and finally 144.

Every IP address is also divided into two sections that define your network and your computer (also known as your host). The first part of an IP address is used as a network address, and the last part as a host address. For example, if you take my IP address again: 76.21.2.144 and divide it into these two parts, 76.21.2 is the network, and 144 is the host. If I add another computer to my home network, it will have a different host part, for example 145, but the network part (76.21.2) would stay the same.

IP addresses, hosts, octets, etc., can become confusing, but just remember that the IP address simply provides your computer with a unique address (remember the post office example) so other devices on the network can communicate with it.

There a lot more to understanding networking concepts and we've only just scratched the surface. If you'd like a more thorough explanation, Microsoft has a great article called "Understanding TCP/IP addressing and subnetting basics" that is worth a read.[xliii] There are also countless books and online articles discussing the subject. Just use your favorite search engine to search for "basic networking concepts."

The Internet Protocol has evolved over the years, and most of the Internet uses a version of IP known as IPv4, or IP version 4.[xliv] There is a more recent version that the Internet is slowly moving to, known as *IPv6*, but we'll get to that a little later.

This is worth mentioning because we are running into an issue with IPv4. While the current networking model has served us well for decades, we now have a problem. There are billions and billions of new things being added to the Internet and the Internet is running out of available addresses (or address space). This is because with IPv4 there are approximately only 4.3 billion numbers (or addresses) available.

Why is this? IPv4 is based on 32 bits. As we know, each bit can only have one of two values – it is either a 0 or a 1. The total possible number of values are 2 (a zero or a one) raised to the power of 32 (2^{32}), which is 4,294,967,296 to be precise; just shy of 4.3 billion.

Each thing connected to the Internet requires its own IP address. (There are some ways around this as you'll see shortly). So, in theory we could connect 4,294,967,296 things to the Internet and be fine. However, there are about ½ million addresses reserved[xlv], which now leaves us with 3.7 billion public addresses.

Now at this point you might be thinking, "hang on a second, I've read recently that there are 20 billion things connected to the Internet, how can that be if there only about 3.7 billion addresses available?" Well, networking engineers saw this problem coming some time ago, and developed technologies such as NAT (network address translation)[xlvi], which in one variant essentially hides multiple devices behind a single IP address. This is known as one-to-many NAT. This is useful for security, as well as scaling. Think of it this way. You might have 10 devices in your home all connected to the Internet, but inside your home they all use private IP addresses, but share a single public address. Your networking device in your home handles the translation between the two. While an oversimplification of how this works, it illustrates one of the ways in which we have been able to scale the finite number of available IP addresses.

As an analogy, think about a family who all live in the same house. All of them can be reached with the same address. They do not all need separate addresses. One-to-many NAT is similar in concept to this. Multiple people living in a private house with one address that is public.

These sorts of techniques can only serve us for so long, so the networking industry has been transitioning to a new version of IP, known as IP version 6, or IPv6.[xlvii] IPv6 is based on a 128-bit scheme, which allows for a significantly larger number of addresses. With IPv6 there are 2^128 (2 to the power of 128) addresses, or 340,282,366,920,938,463,463,374,607,431,768,211,456 IPv6 addresses!

If you were to say this number out loud correctly, you would read it as 340 undecillion, 282 decillion, 366 nonillion, 920 octillion, 938 septillion, 463 sextillion, 463 quintillion, 374 quadrillion, 607 trillion, 431 billion, 768 million, 211 thousand and 456. It's a big number.

Along with significantly more available addresses, IPv6 also uses a new syntax. For example, my IPv6 address is currently 2601:647:4d01:55ee:58b4:912:8ece:44cd. While that is clearly challenging for a human to remember, it is trivial for a machine to recognize.

There are enough IPv6 addresses for every grain of sand on every beach on this planet to have trillions of addresses each. Every star in the known universe could have trillions of addresses with IPv6.

According to Steve Leibson, who identifies himself as "occasional docent at the Computer History Museum," we could "assign an IPV6 address to every atom on the surface of the earth, and still have enough addresses left to do another 100+ earths."[xlviii]

The industry is transitioning to IPv6, but it will take some time. According to the Internet Society's State of IPv6 Deployment 2018 report[xlix], "Over 25% of all Internet-connected networks advertise IPv6 connectivity." It also states that "Google reports 49 countries deliver more than 5% of traffic over IPv6, with new countries joining all the time" and "Google reports 24 countries whose IPv6 traffic exceeds 15%."

The Internet has grown enormously since the early days of the ARPANET. The ARPANET was formally decommissioned on February 28, 1990.

Vinton Cert[l], a well-known computer scientist and considered the "father of the Internet" wrote "Requiem of the ARPANET"[li] (the full text can be found via link in the endnote) in honor of the system.

It was the first, and being first, was best,

but now we lay it down to ever rest.
Now pause with me a moment, shed some tears.
For auld lang syne, for love, for years and years
of faithful service, duty done, I weep.
Lay down thy packet, now, O friend, and sleep.

There are no shortages of books or online material discussing the origin of the Internet, but I've briefly covered it here to set the stage for what is about to come. It may be hard to believe as it's so ingrained in our world, but we are still in the early days of the Internet. Like the ARPANET that came before, the Internet will continue to evolve. Early work on a Quantum Internet[lii] has already begun which may once again transform how we communicate and share.

3. THE CLOUD

"Clouds come floating into my life, no longer to carry rain or usher storm, but to add color to my sunset sky."
- Rabindranath Tagore. Poet, musician and artist. 1861 - 1941

The Internet has become synonymous with the cloud. It's not uncommon to hear the phrase "it's on the Internet", but more and more we hear the phrase "it's in the cloud." The cloud is a key enabler for the Internet of Intelligent Things because as we place more "intelligence" in the cloud, any device with a connection to the cloud can take advantage of that "intelligence." We'll learn more about that "intelligence" shortly, but as a quick example, imagine that a company has developed some clever technology that can recognize faces in an image or video. In addition, they've made that technology freely available for anyone who wants to use it. Now, any device with a camera that has a connection to the Internet can take advantage of that service. This means that your front door camera or security camera could automatically take action based on whether or not it recognized a particular face, perhaps unlocking the front door if it knew it was you.

As we place more and more "intelligent" services in the cloud, connected devices can take advantage of this "intelligence." This leads to an Internet of Intelligent Things.

Well, what exactly is the cloud, how is it different from the Internet, and why is everything moving to the cloud?

While you may assume the Internet and the cloud are the same thing, it is actually possible to use the Internet without using cloud services at all. For example, you could use the Internet to download software or send an e-mail, all without using the cloud, although it is becoming more difficult to do so. The cloud is a shortened term for cloud computing, which refers to a number of technologies that ultimately deal with getting software or computing resources delivered over the Internet as a service. "As a service" is the key phrase here and is what differentiates cloud computing from other computing models and other forms of internet activity. Cloud computing emerged in the 2000s and has now become the standard model for how we use computing resources. The cloud metaphor is credited to David Hoffman, a General Magic communications employee.[liii] In the early days of the Arpanet, a cloud symbol was used to represent networks of computing equipment, and later a cloud symbol was used to represent a network on telephone networks. It has since evolved to illustrate an arbitrary collection of computing or networking equipment whose specific architecture is irrelevant whereas the more important service is emphasized.

There are primarily four types of services delivered over the Internet as cloud computing services. They are:

1. Software as a service (SaaS): This is an application (or more typically, access to an application) delivered over the Internet, usually as a subscription. The benefit is that no application needs to be installed locally on your computer, or if it does it is usually a very lightweight downloadable application such as a "plug-in[liv]" for your web browser. Examples of these are services like Google Apps (word processing, spreadsheets, presentations, storage), or Zendesk, which is a cloud-based customer service and support ticketing platform that websites use when you create a support ticket.
2. Platform as a Service (PaaS). These services typically offer all the tools and technologies you need to build your own cloud-based applications. This includes the runtime platforms like Java and .Net (programming frameworks). Examples include services like Microsoft Azure, and Salesforce.com's Heroku.
3. Infrastructure as a Service (IaaS). These services provide the computing, storage, and networking equipment needed to host your own applications, and set up the hardware and provide the necessary tools to make installing software and applications much easier. Amazon AWS (Amazon Web Services) is one of the largest examples in this category.
4. Some cloud providers mentioned, provide both PaaS and IaaS as one service, so you have one stop shopping for all your cloud development needs. These services also offer tools to monitor the health of your applications and infrastructure as well as tools to automatically scale (grow as demand dictates) your applications and infrastructure.

There are also different types of clouds such as public clouds, private clouds, even hybrid clouds. You choose the one that works best for your needs. No matter the cloud service you use, it's all about having someone else handle the infrastructure or applications so you can focus on what is important or unique to your business. In today's world it is not uncommon to use a service to take care of something we'd rather not do ourselves or have the skills or tools to do. Dry cleaning, oil changes, home repair, etc. are all examples of services others provide. Cloud computing is no different in the technology world.

There are many benefits to cloud computing and its popularity is growing. Some of these benefits include:

- The cloud provider can support more customers with less resources. These resources may be people, hardware, real estate, etc. It's all about achieving economies of scale. A core premise of cloud computing is about sharing of resources to achieve these economies. This is a similar model to a water or electric company. Consider, for example a power plant that generates electricity for tens of thousands of customers. Having the power generation centralized means that less people are needed to run a single power plant vs. having dozens of smaller distributed power plants. Power plants need a power plant operator – someone who controls the systems. A single power plant needs only one or two of these resources, whereas a dozen power plants might need twenty of these resources. Centralizing management and generation of something requires less resources.
- Developing in the cloud enables companies to focus on their applications and get their applications to market quickly. With a few clicks on a web page, an individual or a company can set-up a massively scalable computing infrastructure that might otherwise take months or be cost-prohibitive.
- Cloud Storage allows companies and users to get to their data from anywhere. Because it's in the cloud, content is more easily accessible. In addition to access, cloud storage companies will take care of backing up your data for you. Example of these types of companies or services include Box, Dropbox, and Google Drive.
- Typically cloud computing is cheaper. If you compare the capital costs (fixed, one-time expenses) of buying hardware, and then having the personnel to set it up, install software, and maintain it, cloud computing starts to look very attractive. And with cloud computing providers, the

- cost of new hardware and software upgrades are included in the price so it's one less thing for a company to worry about.
- And finally, someone else maintains the infrastructure so you don't have to hire people to manage the computers, add disks, add memory, fix problems, etc. You can focus on what's important to your business. In the business world this is known as core vs. context.[lv] This is a distinction that separates the activities that a company does into two buckets – one that creates true differentiation (core) versus the things a company needs to do to operate (context).

In the "old days" companies used dedicated hardware that was specific to them, no one else could use it, and they paid for it whether it was being used or not. With cloud computing, infrastructure is shared in a secure way. This is great from a business perspective as businesses don't need to invest in infrastructure that they would have to maintain. They don't need to hire staff to support or upgrade the infrastructure periodically. This is all done by the cloud provider and customers simply pay a subscription fee.

You likely use numerous cloud services every day and may not realize it. Your email, Amazon, Apple iCloud, Spotify, and YouTube are all examples of cloud services.

Many of the cloud services are known as *elastic* services as they can grow or shrink as needed based on demand.[lvi] For example, perhaps during the holidays a company expects a lot more customers on their website buying products. With a cloud solution, the infrastructure can automatically grow to accommodate the increased demand, and then shrink back down after the holiday season. The customer only pays for what they used. This elasticity of the cloud is one of its characteristics that makes it so attractive.

We've come to expect a lot from cloud providers and there are now countless offerings for both business and consumers. Like much of the Internet, cloud computing had an interesting beginning.

In the very early days of computing, computing resources, such as those in a university or company were fixed. In other words, someone sat at a computer terminal that was physically connected to the computer and performed whatever task they needed to accomplish. While the individual was preforming the task, other users could not use the same resource. This made computing very expensive and not very efficient. If you were performing a long calculation for example, no one else could use that same resource until you were finished. Later, in the 1960's, technology companies such as IBM and DEC introduced concepts such as time-sharing that reduced the burden.

Time-sharing came from the realization that a single user sitting at a computer was quite inefficient. Most of the time when we sit at a computer, we're not actually doing anything, at least from the computer's perspective. Perhaps we're reading something on the screen, thinking about what we're about to type next, etc. During this time, the computer spends a lot of time being idle. It occurred to engineers that this idle time could be given to other users to perform their tasks. This was known as multi-tasking. In a time-sharing system, multi-tasking is a bit of an illusion. Multiple people can use the same computer and it appears from an individual's perspective that the computer is dedicated just to them. Behinds the scenes however, the computer is pausing and resuming programs during the idle times. This is an over-simplification of what's really going on behind the scenes, but it illustrates the general idea.

Allowing many users to interact with a single computer at the same time considerably lowered the cost of providing computing capabilities. It led to more interactive applications and was a major shift in the history of computing. It ultimately became the basis for how we use computing resources today. Imagine if while you used the Internet no one else could. While that might be fun to ponder, it would significantly limit the usefulness of the Internet.

We have come a long way from rudimentary multi-tasking. Today's computers use many sophisticated techniques to appear to do a lot of things at once. It is typical for today's computing devices to have multiple cores in the processor. A core is part of the processor that performs calculations independent of the other cores. In turn, the cores themselves can execute multiple threads (part of a program) at the same time. Even some of the high-end mobile phones on the market today sport eight cores. Significant computing power is no longer limited to the computer on your desk. That computer in your pocket is billions of times faster than these early computers, and yet ironically has a single user – you.

You may be wondering why the Internet history lesson, and what does this have to do with the Internet of Intelligent things? As we'll learn, more and more services are moving to the cloud, and more and more things are tapping into those services. The cloud is a key component of the Internet of Intelligent Things.

4. THE HISTORY OF THE INTERNET OF THINGS

"It's the little details that are vital. Little things make big things happen."
- John Wooden – 10-time NCAA Championship-winning coach and member of the Basketball Hall of Fame

In March of 2004, I wrote a paper called "Micronets, the Incredible Shrinking Network" where I stated, "In the next decade we will see a network that will dwarf the Internet. This network will be everywhere. It will be in your clothes, in your car, in your jewelry, on your food, on the battlefield, and in the air. This is a network that could literally get under your skin. While RFID[lvii] (radio-frequency identification) will be the initial catalyst for this new network, RFID is just the beginning."

I went on to say "The growth of the Micronet will not be without its challenges; issues around privacy, environment impacts, and health concerns will all need to be addressed. The Micronet will grow rapidly however, and in following in its larger cousins' footsteps, the Micronet will have as broad applicability as the Internet has; arguably more, due to its diminutive size. There are huge opportunities in all industry verticals; transportation, retail, healthcare, and manufacturing, to name a few."

I was not clever enough at the time to use the moniker "The Internet of Things" (although I did later coin the term "The Internet of Everything" which I'll cover in the next chapter) and instead I used the term "Micronets" to illustrate the departure of a monolithic network.

While I was not the first to write about IoT, I understood its impact and promise early on. I closed the paper with "Micronets is a big small thing waiting to happen." While we use a different, more applicable term today, the sentiment was the same. IoT was indeed a big small thing waiting to happen.

Kevin Ashton, while the Executive Director of Auto-ID Labs at MIT, was the first to describe the Internet of Things and is credited with the term. Born in Birmingham, UK, (only a few miles from where yours truly was born) Ashton was working as an assistant brand manager at Procter & Gamble in 1997 when he became interested in using RFID to help manage P&G's supply chain. In 1999 he made a presentation for Procter & Gamble and stated.[lviii]

"Today computers, and, therefore, the Internet, are almost wholly dependent on human beings for information. Nearly all of the roughly 50 petabytes (a petabyte is 1,024 terabytes) of data available on the Internet were first captured and created by human beings by typing, pressing a record button, taking a digital picture or scanning a bar code. The problem is, people have limited time, attention, and accuracy. All of which means they are not very good at capturing data about things in the real world. If we had computers that knew everything there was to know about things, using data they gathered without any help from us, we would be able to track and count everything and greatly reduce waste, loss and cost. We would know when things needed replacing, repairing or recalling and whether they were fresh or past their best."

Kevin Ashton believed RFID was a prerequisite for the Internet of Things. While RFID has its limitations, it was indeed just the beginning of a much larger shift.

Finding a comprehensive, consistent definition for the Internet of things is surprisingly challenging. A simple Google search will yield many different definitions. I have been in more than one debate with those that think they have a very clear definition.

One definition is: "Sensors and actuators embedded in physical objects are linked through wired and wireless networks." Another which expands on it slightly is: "Sensors and actuators embedded in physical objects are linked through wired and wireless networks, often using the same Internet Protocol (IP) that connects the Internet."[lix]

I've had discussions with some that staunchly believe that because the Internet of Things rests upon the Internet, it must share the same protocols to be truly considered an IoT thing. There are many devices that we now colloquially refer to as an IoT device, such as a wearable, door lock, a smoke alarm, etc., that do not use IP. They use other protocols such as Bluetooth, Z-Wave,

Zigbee instead, as these are often more suited for the application. These alternative protocols use less energy and are more *lightweight* than IP. Some would argue that these are not true IoT devices. I would argue differently. My definition for the Internet of Things is simple: if a thing connects to, and/or relies on the Internet directly, or indirectly, then I think it's reasonable to consider it an IoT device.

Another way to think about it, is that when the Internet serves more things than it does people, one could argue that the Internet is an Internet of Things. In 2010, I calculated approximately how many things were connected to the Internet, and how many people were connected to the Internet. I then determined that the Internet of things was born sometime between 2008 and 2009 by that measure. You can read more about this in the paper, "The Internet of Things:

How the Next Evolution of the Internet Is Changing Everything."[lx]

You might be asking yourself, "what's the difference between my computer connected to the Internet, and an IoT device - aren't they just the same thing?" The primary difference is that IoT devices contain sensors while also being connected to the Internet. For example, the wearable you may have on your wrist contains a tiny sensor called an accelerometer that measures movement. This movement can be translated into physical activity, which can then be shared online. Of course, modern wearables may contain more than just an accelerometer, they may contain a heart rate sensor, a galvanic skin response sensor (helps to measure emotional states, such as stress), a glucose monitor, and more. Regardless of what they measure, it is just data to a computer, which can be analyzed and shared. The key difference here is that IoT devices are computers with sensors that are connected to the Internet.

While there are some subtleties to the different definitions of the Internet of things, generally speaking IoT devices differentiate themselves from typical Internet devices through the addition of some sort of sensing mechanism.

Over time the definition will become less and less important and will likely evolve to simply mean "things connected to the Internet."

IoT shares some of the same challenges that the Internet did in the early days. In my own home for example, I have dozens of things that work really well as discrete things but do not work very well as part of a larger system.

In my home I have a connected thermostat, a connected door lock, connected lights, as well as a host of other miscellaneous devices. The challenge is that they are all made by different companies and all work differently. Each is managed by its own application, and at a technical level many of them use different protocols and standards like Zigbee, Z-Wave, Wi-Fi to name a few.[lxi] This is no longer an unusual scenario. Countless homes use these types of technologies hoping to get some benefit from these devices.

Therein lies part of the challenge. I, like many others, do not want these devices to just be standalone devices, we want them to work as a system.

Consider the act of leaving your house. When I leave the house, I want the house to act as a cohesive system. I want the front door to lock, the temperature to turn down, and the lights to turn off, all automatically, and intelligently, all because the house knew I had left. I do not want to have to jump from app to app to app to control all of these devices, I want them to work together – just like Sally does.

It turns out that something so simple from the user's perspective is quite difficult to do technically, because all these things speak different protocols, have different APIs (application programming interfaces - a way to talk to these things programmatically), and use different standards.

This was so reminiscent of the Internet's early days, and a problem I had observed while at Cisco, that after almost 24 years I decided to leave Cisco to start a company to address these issues. In 2014, I co-founded a company called Stringify. Our mission was to build, in essence, a multiprotocol router of sorts for the Internet of things. This was not to be another hardware device, but rather a cloud-based service that let the end-user focus on building great experiences with the things they had, instead of worrying about the things themselves. When the company was acquired in 2017[lxii], we were supporting hundreds of different types of discrete things on the platform that a user could mix and match to create great experiences without worrying about the protocol, the standard, or who made the thing. Stringify no longer exists as a company but there are a number of other alternatives such as IFTTT ("If This, Then That").[lxiii] We are also seeing more of these automations being embedded into operating system such as iOS, the operating system that powers Apple's line of iPhones.[lxiv]

I believe that as AI becomes more prevalent, your home will simply take care of these automation tasks for you. AI will learn from your habits and adapt your home to your needs without your intervention.

Let's say you go to bed around the same time each night, and before you go to bed you turn off the lights and lock the front door. Perhaps one night you're particularly tired and you forget to lock the front door. An intelligent home in the future will recognize that and lock the door for you, automatically.

Therein I believe lies the great power of IoT. While we often focus on the things themselves, the things are simply a means to an end. A connected light for example, is a means to save energy and to improve security. A connected wearable is a means towards a fitness or health goal.

Connecting these devices to one another via the Internet was a powerful first step. As we place more "intelligence" in the cloud these connected things can also tap into that intelligence. This is the dawn of the Internet of Intelligent Things.

That same light bulb could query the power company to see if the grid is being overloaded and adjust its energy usage accordingly. It might also check with the other devices in your home to see if you are home. If you are not, it might decide to turn itself off to save energy.

That same wearable might talk to your bathroom scale and encourage you to work out a few minutes longer if you've gained an extra pound. It might talk to your connected dinnerware to see what you've eaten for dinner and adjust your workout appropriately.

As you are starting to see, the Internet of Intelligent Things differs significantly from the Internet of Things in that it's the addition of "intelligence" that makes "dumb" things smart. As everyday things get connected to the Internet, and as more and more "intelligent" services get added to the cloud, things adapt and adjust in entirely new ways. New capabilities and new business models emerge. The Internet of Things will look primitive relative to the Internet of Intelligent Things.

It is not about the things, and it's not just what you can do with the things. It is what the things ultimately do for people. Technology does not exist for technologies sake; technology exists to benefit humanity.

In the next chapter will expand upon the Internet of Things and talk about why the person is at the center of it all.

5. THE INTERNET OF EVERYTHING

"Everything has beauty, but not everyone sees it."
- Confucius (Kong Qiu) – Chinese philosopher, teacher and political figure

In 2010 I gave a presentation at Cisco. On my first slide I had a picture of a cow, a tree, and a shoe. I asked the audience, "what do these three things have in common?" These were of course just three examples of things that were getting connected to the Internet.

At the time of the presentation, the cow referred to the work that a Dutch company called Sparked was doing connecting their livestock to the Internet. By adding sensors to livestock, you could track their health, feeding habits, and even determine if a cow was getting ready to give birth. By connecting the sensors then, to the Internet, you could give the farmer timely notice if any of his livestock required attention. Connected livestock will be the standard way farmers manage their herds.

The tree referred to a tree in Brussels that had sensors on it and was in turn connected to the Internet. The tree could Tweet to let its followers know environmental conditions. It was essentially a proxy for the environment. (It's an interesting world we are creating when we are now following trees on Twitter.)

And finally, the shoe referred to a shoe sensor that Nike had just developed allowing the wearer to track their fitness activity. Today we typically wear fitness sensors on our wrists, but the functionality is similar.

These vastly different things all had one thing in common which today is quite obvious. They all use the Internet to share information that they had gathered with their sensors.

Now with tens of billions of things connected to the Internet, examples such as these are becoming less and less unique, but at the time it highlighted a fundamental shift in the use of the Internet.

The Internet was evolving. This was more than just connecting things to the Internet; this was about connecting every *thing*.

It was during this time I was credited with coining the phrase the Internet of Everything.

Prior to this timeframe, the typical things connected to the Internet were networking devices and computers. This was the beginning of a departure where normal day to day things were being connected. These things benefited everyone, not just scientists and engineers. The data that they were creating was growing rapidly (which we'll see in an upcoming chapter), and the new types of business processes that could be developed as a result were redefining industries.

Later, Cisco provided a clearer definition to the Internet of Everything: the intersection of people, process, data and things.[lxv] The emphasis was no longer just on the things.

It is easy to get caught up in the sheer number of things getting connected to the Internet. 10 billion, 20 billion, 50 billion and beyond. But it's not just about the number of things, it's the types of things; it's the next tree, the next cow, the next shoe. The things that we cannot yet envision are those that excite me most. With the Internet of Everything, things that were silent will have a voice.

6. IT'S THE CONNECTIONS THAT MATTER

"**It's not what you know, it's who you know.**"
- English Proverb

Imagine you are shipwrecked on an isolated island. You have no communication with the outside world. You have no Internet, no phone, no way to speak to anyone. Everything you need to know to survive depends upon what you already know. How long would you last?

Now, consider the same scenario, yet this time you have a mobile phone. You can call anyone in the world for advice. This dramatically changes your odds of survival.

A connection changes everything.

We rely on connections to be productive and strive in today's society. You've no doubt heard the expression "it's not what you know, it's who you know." These are connections. They are all around us and yet we often take them for granted. Our connections in the business world help us be productive. Family connections give us a sense of belonging. Our houses are connected to the rest of the world via telecommunications connections. Infrastructure connections such as utilities and roadways bring services to our homes.

Connectivity is integral to everything we do.

This simple, yet powerful construct applies to things, too. A thing by itself has limited utility, but once connected to the Internet, it has the potential to be connected to every other thing.

Consider the thermostat on the wall. It's useful in that it can control your in-home heating and cooling, but that's where its value ends. Now give that same thermostat a connection to the Internet and it becomes exponentially more useful. It can be controlled remotely. It can connect to weather services to make smarter decisions on when to operate. It can connect to utilities to determine the optimal time to run to save energy. It can connect to your other connected devices, such as your car, so it can turn itself down when you leave the house. There are many other examples, but you get the point.

Giving a thing a connection fundamentally changes the utility of that thing. It also allows that thing to contribute to the decision making of other things.

Adding a single thing to the Internet (or any network for that matter) increases the device count, but the connections it creates grows even more significantly.

The math formula to calculate the connections is pretty straightforward. It is:

$$\frac{n(n-1)}{2}$$

Figure 3 - CONNECTIONS FORMULA

This simply states that if you have n number of things, apply this formula and it will tell you how many connections they share.

Let's begin with the simplest example: two things connected to one another. If we apply this formula, it looks like this:

$$\frac{2(2-1)}{2}$$

Figure 4 - CONNECTIONS FORMULA EXAMPLE

And the result of the calculation is clearly 1. You didn't need a formula to calculate that. Two things clearly share just 1 connection. Let's see what the results are with a few more examples.

Number of Things	Number of Connections
2	1
5	10
10	45
100	4,950
1,000	499,500
10,000	49,995,000

Figure 5 - THINGS VS CONNECTIONS

Notice how the number of connections grow dramatically relative to the number of things.

Visually, this formula looks like this:

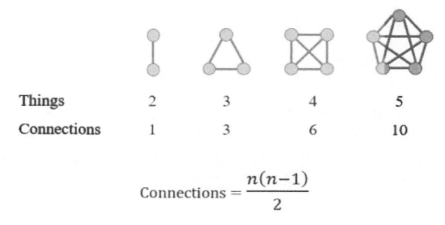

$$\text{Connections} = \frac{n(n-1)}{2}$$

Figure 6 – VISUAL REPRESENTATION OF THINGS TO CONNECTIONS

This formula calculates how many connections result from a given number of things. These types of calculations are used in graph theory and computer science for numerous applications. For example, when using social media sites to connect with family and friends, social network analysis is used to understand relationships between people and social structures.[lxvi]

It's quite easy to see how quickly the number of connections grows when only a few more things are connected. With only 100 things, the number of connections nears 5,000. Where this becomes staggering is when you connect a lot of things.

As we'll see in the "Power in Numbers" chapter, I previously estimated that there would be about 27 billion things connected to the Internet by 2020. This leads to a staggering number of connections.

Number of Things	Number of Connections
27,000,000,000	364,499,999,986,500,000,000

Figure 7 – CONNECTONS FOR 27 BILLION THINGS

That's 364 quintillion connections. Clearly, the number of connections dwarf the number of things.

Connecting every thing to every other thing wouldn't make practical sense, but this simple thought experiment serves to illustrate how powerful connecting things to one another is. Even if a given thing were connected to a very small percentage of the other connected things, this is still a massive number of connections. The takeaway here is that more connections means more capabilities.

Think about how much smarter your home could become when all the things in your home are connected together instead of them being disparate devices. Now consider how this changes cities and even countries on a grander scale. Connecting things to many other things and services is powerful.

From the local neighborhood to the entire country, the Internet of Intelligent Things makes our world more dynamic and adaptive. Imagine for example if homes could talk to one another. Let's say your neighbor had a break-in. That home could alert other homes in the neighborhood to lock their doors or look out for suspicious individuals. It might automatically broadcast a photo of a suspicious person to the neighbor's cameras to be on the lookout for that person.

Intelligent sensors that detect an earthquake in a country might warn nearby cities of an impending shake giving them time to warn inhabitants or automatically shutting off gas lines to prevent fires.

Homes, buildings, cities, and countries could act as dynamic, living, breathing systems that adapt in real-time to different scenarios.

The connections matter, but the quality of the connections matters too. Not just the network quality of course, but the quality of the things or services being connected.

Using the earlier thermostat example, consider if the thermostat relied on weather data from a weather service. If that weather service was unreliable, the quality of the data was poor, or the service itself was unreliable, that limits the thermostat's value as a connected device.

This is an important consideration as we connect billions of things to the Internet and many of them together, relying on each other. If the quality of the connections is poor, then the whole system suffers. If the quality of the connections is good, then the whole system benefits. The quality of the connections improves when intelligence is added. This is because things can adapt, adjust, and make smarter decisions because of the intelligence services the connect to. Improving the intelligence of each thing in a network, increases the value of the network overall.

For a moment, imagine if you wanted to take a trip to a country you had never visited. The only resource you have is your neighbor Bob. Bob has never travelled anywhere and is a bit of a loner. It's unlikely you would get good advice or information from Bob. Instead, you decide to talk to your other neighbor, Alice. Alice is a world traveler; she's visited the country you are interested in numerous times. She's friends with lots of other travelers; she has a rich network of friends. It's clear which person you would benefit from most.

The value of the network increases based upon the quality of information your network provides. The Internet of Intelligent Things is no different. The better, and richer, the sources of information, the better the overall network.

7. SECURITY AND PRIVACY

"For me, privacy and security are really important. We think about it in terms of both: You can't have privacy without security."
- Larry Page. Co-founder, Google.

One cannot have a discussion about connected things without addressing security and privacy. They are both so intertwined that I often refer to them as the two halves of the same coin. If you compromise one, you inevitably compromise the other.

As we connect more and more things to the Internet, the opportunity for security and privacy breaches grow, too.

However, the Internet of Intelligent Things could help with security and privacy. No longer are connections simply "dumb" connections routing information to and fro. Now connected things could potentially query other things to check the validity of that service before connecting to it. Things could warn other things when they detect an attack so those other things could block the attacker. The Internet of Intelligent Things is certainly not a panacea for the realities of Internet security threats, but it offers an opportunity to do more.

There have been no shortages of stories in the media about *hackers*[lxvii] that have broken into websites or compromised connected devices that have resulted in personal information, such as credit cards or passwords, being stolen as well as services interrupted.

In 2016, the Internet saw one of its largest attacks to date. A massive, international cyberattack "took control of smart home devices, such as security cameras, effectively turning them into zombie machines that directed Internet traffic to take down popular websites like Netflix and Twitter.[lxviii]" This was known as the Mirai botnet attack. According to a person who published the Mirai code, he claimed that the botnet had controlled over 380,000 devices.[lxix]

Even unlikely devices not properly secured can be a target for hackers to gain access. In 2017 a connected fish tank provided hackers the access they needed to hack into a casino.[lxx] The fish tank was connected to the Internet to automatically feed the fish and keep their environment comfortable. It was the weak link in the casino's security and likely not given a second thought.

Attacks are increasing in quantity and scale. Kaspersky Labs is a multinational cybersecurity and anti-virus provider headquartered in Moscow, Russia and operated by a holding company in the United Kingdom. According to a recent Kaspersky Lab report.[lxxi] Q1 of 2018 saw a significant increase in both the total number of attacks, and the duration of those attacks, compared to Q4 of 2017.

Some highlights of the report include:
- *In Q1 2018, the longest DDoS attack lasted 297 hours, or more than 12 days.*
- *DDoS botnets attacked online resources in 79 countries in Q1 2018.*

Before we move on, let's take a moment to explain some of the jargon being used and terms you'll come across as you read about Internet attacks. (The more you know, the better you can protect yourself and your things).

Hacker

You may think you already know what a hacker is – it's someone who breaks into systems to do bad things. That hasn't always been the case, however. In fact, until relatively recently a hacker, or more specifically a computer hacker, was a positive moniker. They were a "skilled computer expert that uses their technical knowledge to overcome a problem."[lxxii] Now the mainstream usage of "hacker" mostly refers to computer criminals, due to the mass media usage of the word since the 1980s.[lxxiii] When I studied computer science in the '80's, being called a hacker was considered a compliment, and in some cases, the positive form of the word "hack" still exists in some contexts today, as with the term "lifehack" to describe a clever technique for dealing with an everyday task or problem.

Why do hackers break into (hack) systems? There are a number of motives that typically range from financial gain, such as obtaining credit card numbers, to fame and prestige within the hacker community. In addition, hacking is not limited to individuals. Companies may try to hack into other companies to acquire information on their competitors, such as products being developed. State-sponsored attacks may provide nation states with both wartime and intelligence collection options.[lxxiv]

Bot

A Bot, also known as an Internet Bot, or web robot, is a software application that runs automated tasks, also known as scripts, over the Internet.[lxxv]

Bots often run tasks that are highly repetitive, trying the same set of things over and over again. Not all bots are bad however, in fact many are quite useful. One of the largest use of bots is in web spidering, also known as web crawling, in which automated scripts fetch content from other sites in order to build a list of pages from those sites. This is what enables search results to be returned so quickly when you perform a search on your favorite search engine.

It may surprise you to know that more than half of all web traffic is made up of bots[lxxvi] and some of these bots are indeed bad. Some bots are used to populate social media sites with "fake news" to influence public opinion or elections. In 2016, Twitter bots spread "fake news" before, during, and after the 2016 U.S. presidential election. By creating more "fake news" than real news, users were biased into thinking the "fake news" was real, thereby influencing them.[lxxvii] Bots are simply automated tasks, by themselves they are neither good or bad, and like most technology, it is how they are used.

Botnet

A botnet is a network of bots – hence the name *bot-net*. The software (the bot) typically resides on numerous Internet-connected devices and may be used to perform malicious attacks.

Botnets can be used to perform distributed denial-of-service attacks (see below), steal data, send spam, and allow the attacker to access the device and its connection.[lxxviii]

DoS

A Denial of Service is an attack in which the perpetrator attempts to make a service unavailable to others by disrupting that service. There are a variety of techniques to do this such as a distributed denial of service (see below). The web site (or service) often cannot distinguish between a legitimate request or one made by a bot, so it handles both. By flooding a web site or service with requests, the service is denied to others, hence, the name, Denial of Service.

DDoS

This is similar to a Denial of Service attack except that it is distributed, allowing for a lot more devices to perform the attack as well as making it much harder to shut them down. These devices could be distributed geographically, even in other countries, so shutting them down is challenging. This is typically a large-scale attack where the perpetrator may use thousands of compromised devices (possibly running bots) to flood a site or service with network traffic. Like the denial of service attack, because the service is so busy processing these incoming requests, it is unable to handle legitimate requests and the service is made unavailable. Think about using your favorite website. Normally the website can easily handle your request. But, if the website is flooded with thousands of requests a second, it is so busy trying to process requests that the service is unavailable to others. It also has no way of knowing what is legitimate (your request) vs. what is an attack. It has to handle all requests and in doing so, service is denied to you.

You might be wondering, why not simply ignore these "fake" requests? As mentioned, the devices that have been compromised originate from many different sources, sometimes geographically, therefore it is very difficult to filter them out from legitimate user requests. In addition, DDoS attacks may involve the forging of sender IP addresses. This is known as IP address spoofing. IP address spoofing means that the device may be impersonating another, possible legitimate IP address. This makes identifying the attacker much more difficult. Although routers can be configured to block certain IP addresses, when an IP address is spoofed, it becomes challenging to know what a legitimate request is. DDoS attacks can last for hours or even days, significantly disrupting a business.

If connected devices are not well protected, for example with strong, non-default passwords, a malicious hacker could compromise that device, install a bot on it and perform a botnet attack resulting in a denial of service. IoT devices that you own could be used in these types of attacks.[lxxix]

You may be thinking that while this is interesting background information, what does it have to do with me, or the things I have in my own home. Surely, I won't be a victim of DoS or DDoS attack?

While you may not be a victim personally, the devices in your home could indeed be used to attack someone else. In fact, one of the largest DDoS attacks occurred in 2016 and used hijacked IoT devices such as cameras, lightbulbs, and thermostats.[lxxx]

If not secured correctly, connected devices in your home could be used to compromise your network and potentially steal your personal information. As we learned earlier, the CEO of a cybersecurity firm, Darktrace told the story of how "hackers once stole a casino's high-roller database through a thermometer in the lobby fish tank."[lxxxi] The thermometer could just as easily be a connected device in your home. As this point you might be questioning the benefits of connected things at all. Don't be. The benefits significantly outweigh the risks, and as we'll see shortly, some common sense and some good security practices can address many of the security risks.

There is obviously much more to Internet security and attacks, and these are just a few examples that hackers can use to compromise systems. Perhaps more worryingly however, is that many experts believe that the worst is yet to come.[lxxxii] As we connect more and more of our infrastructure (cities, power plants, water systems, etc.) to the Internet, strong security becomes more important than ever. It is one thing to compromise a website, it is another issue completely when a power plant, utility, or even a city is compromised.

By now, you may be asking yourself what can be done about this? This is not a simple issue, and hackers use sophisticated attacks – some technological, some social engineering[lxxxiii] to get into systems, yet there are some simple things you can do to help protect yourself and your devices.

One of the easiest things you personally can do is to use strong passwords for your connected devices and the sites you visit. Your security is only as strong as your weakest password. Remember the connected fish tank example earlier? A weak link in the security chain caused a lot of headaches for the casino. You may think that changing your default password on a connected device you own doesn't matter all that much, but since everyday devices can be compromised and used in attacks like DDoS, securing that device can make a big difference.

SplashData, a company that deals with computer security, has published a ranking of the worst 100 passwords used in 2017. They estimate that almost 10% of people used at least one of these 100 worst passwords and almost 3% of people used the worst password ever. Can you guess what that worst password is? It's 123456.[lxxxiv] (If you use this as your password, you might want to consider changing it).

There are some excellent security guides online, for example "How to Create Secure And Easy To Remember Passwords."[lxxxv] Having a strong password is your first line of defense.

One of the biggest issues with connected devices is that many of them use well-known default passwords that are never changed by the user. According to a report published by security researchers from Positive Technologies, "just five sets of passwords allow online intruders to access 10% of all the connected IoT devices."[lxxxvi] Think about that – just five sets of passwords allow hackers to access hundreds of millions of connected devices. Said more accurately, if there are 20 billion devices connected to the Internet today, then five sets of passwords allow hackers to access 2 billion connected devices.

According to the report, the five sets of default username and passwords are:

1. support/support
2. admin/admin
3. admin/0000
4. user/user
5. root/12345

If you have not changed the default passwords on your connected devices, now might be a good time. Go ahead, I'll wait.

Not changing the default password is akin to leaving your home with your front door locked but allowing everyone to have a copy of the key to the front door – clearly not very effective.

The Mirai botnet attack I referenced earlier was successful because many of the default passwords had not been changed and those that had still used common usernames and passwords. In fact, the Mirai bot needed only 62 sets of usernames and passwords to create the botnet.[lxxxvii]

While it's easy to blame device manufacturers, we must also shoulder some of the responsibility. We have a responsibility to be educated about the devices we purchase, to change the default passwords, and to use strong password techniques. If we leave our homes with the front door wide open, it's not the house builders' fault.

However, this does not mean easing up on device manufacturers. Demand strong security from them, and if they don't provide it, look elsewhere. There are plenty of alternatives. Before you purchase that next connected device, do your research. Check the manufacturer's website and see how often they provide software updates to the product. Do they talk about security in their documentation? What do others say about the device in product reviews? There are plenty of resources online. A simple Google search for "[device] security issues", where [device] is the product you are considering, should yield a ton of good information.

The same applies for services you use. Check their terms of service – how are they planning on using your data? Is your data stored safely on their site? Ask them how they secure your data and ensure it's safe. As we'll learn later, new legislation such as GDPR (General Data Protection Regulation), as an example, specifies clear guidelines for how data is used and imposes stiff fines for companies that don't comply.

What else can you do? In addition to changing the default credentials and using strong passwords, you should also:

- Keep your devices up to date. Install the latest software updates which often fixes bugs, vulnerabilities, and security issues.
- Download apps from trusted sources. Do your homework, read online reviews and check comments to be sure the applications you are using to manage your connected devices are safe to use.
- Make sure your network is secure – both home and business. Limit who has access to it. Individual devices may be secure, but if your network is insecure, perhaps due to a weak Wi-Fi password, you're inviting issues.
- Educate yourself on the basics of security. There are tons of resources online. Whenever you buy a connected device, be sure you understand how to secure it – it's partly your responsibility.

We've talked quite a bit about security, but what about privacy? When your security is compromised, access to your private information becomes much easier. When your privacy is compromised, accessing your secure things becomes much easier.

We live in an interesting time where so many services are free. Social media, applications, search engines, etc. We have an expectation of privacy, yet we do not pay for many of the services we use, yet someone has to pay salaries, buy equipment, pay for the buildings, etc.

Nothing is free.

The phrase "if you're not paying for it, you're not the customer, you're the product" is not unique to the Internet era yet is very applicable in today's online world.[lxxxviii]

We willingly provide massive amounts of personal information to online services. Every time you take an online quiz on a social media site, you're giving away personal information. Online activity can reveal where we live, who we're married to, how many kids we have, our hobbies, our travel, our current location, the food we eat, what we drive, our sexual & political persuasions, and on and on. We also willingly provide this data in rich photos and video that machine learning is quickly learning to understand.

Even if you are not providing it directly, someone else is. Perhaps someone posted a picture of you or mentioned you in a post. Information about you is everywhere.

In many cases we provide all this for free yet fail to understand what is happening with our data. Who's selling it, who's buying it, what's being done with it. We should not be surprised then when we find out that companies sell our *private* data in order to make revenue. Don't expect something for nothing. You are the product.

We willingly give away massive amounts of information yet are often surprised when some website or service knows so much about us.

Recently my wife and I were talking to our son about a minor chest pain, most likely due to heartburn. There had been a single text message sent on the topic, and the rest of the conversation was by phone. The following day both my wife and I saw ads on different websites advertising heart burn medications. Neither one of us had seen these before. Coincidence, or very thorough data-mining algorithms? Needless to say, we were a little concerned.

Philosophies about data sharing have changed. With the World Wide Web turning 30[lxxxix], a large portion of the population grew up in a time when the Internet always existed. Our attitudes towards privacy have changed. I recall a few years ago, someone made the astute comment that when they grew up, they considered all their personal information to be private and they chose what to give away. Today many consider all information to be public and we choose what to keep private. This is becoming increasingly difficult, and perhaps soon, impossible. Attitudes towards data privacy have changed.

This is not to say that social media is inherently bad, quite the contrary. It allows people to reach out and stay in touch with family and friends from all over the globe. It allows one to get the latest on world news via a click of a mouse or a tap of screen. There are many benefits to social media, and it is having a profound effect on society, but it is important to understand that it often comes with privacy trade-offs.

There are some interesting technologies on the horizon that may very well address the security and privacy shortcomings of IoT. One of these is Blockchain, and a book on IoT would not be complete without at least a brief overview of what it is and its relevance to IoT.

8. BLOCKCHAIN

"Security is, I would say, our top priority because for all the exciting things you will be able to do with computers - organizing your lives, staying in touch with people, being creative - if we don't solve these security problems, then people will hold back."

- Bill Gates, founder of Microsoft

Recently there has been a lot of press about a cryptocurrency called Bitcoin. "A cryptocurrency (or crypto currency) is a digital asset designed to work as a medium of exchange that uses strong cryptography to secure financial transactions, control the creation of additional units, and verify the transfer of assets."[xc] Bitcoin received a lot of attention because of the spectacular growth it achieved in a very short period of time.[xci] In February of 2011, a single Bitcoin was worth exactly one US dollar. Six years later, a single Bitcoin commanded an incredible $19,783.21 when it reached its high in December of 2017. However, this meteoric rise was short lived. Just days later, the cryptocurrency plummeted 30%; one of the biggest market corrections the cryptocurrency market had seen.[xcii]

While the future of Bitcoin and other cryptocurrencies are unknown, the technology that powered it has far-reaching implications. This underlying technology is Blockchain.[xciii]

It's important to note that Bitcoin and Blockchain are not the same thing. While they are sometimes used interchangeably by those without a deeper understanding, they are quite different.

Bitcoin is an electronic currency and like any electronic currency, it requires a way to ensure its transactions are recorded and secure. This is where Blockchain comes in. Blockchain is the underpinning technology that records the Bitcoin transactions. Bitcoin is just one of the many cryptocurrencies as well as other digital assets that make use of Blockchain technology.

The definition of Blockchain can be found in its name. It is quite literally a chain of digital blocks. Each block contains data and one block links to the next block in the chain.

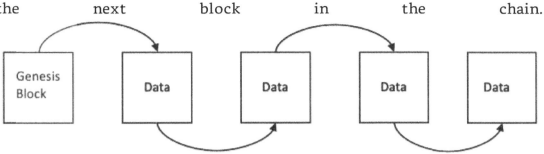

Figure 8 – A SIMPLIFIED BLOCKCHAIN

The first block in the chain is known as the Genesis block. It is also known as Block 0. It is typically hardcoded into the Blockchain software and is the one block that all other blocks can trace their lineage to.

In computer science, first year students will learn about a data structure (data organization model) known as a linked list.[xciv] A linked list is a linear data structure (as opposed to other data structures, such as a tree) where each node is a separate object. Each of these nodes consists of two items, some data, and a link, or reference to the next node. It's a bit like a train where each car contains a payload and is connected or coupled to the next train car. The Blockchain structure is similar to a linked list.

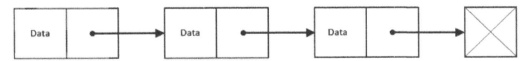

Figure 9 - A LINKED LIST

Before we delve into some of the details behind Blockchain, let's enumerate some of the attributes that makes it attractive as a secure platform:

- Blockchain is decentralized. Each node (a device on a blockchain network) participating in the Blockchain network stores an entire copy of the Blockchain. This makes it very difficult to attack as there is no central place to attack.
- Blockchain is append only, meaning it can only be added to. Once data is written it cannot be changed, updated, or deleted. This creates an immutable record of all the transactions and data. Unlike other data storage systems such as databases, once written to a Blockchain, the data cannot be changed.

- Blockchain can be used to store anything of value that can be digitized. Although blockchain gained its fame initially thanks to Bitcoin, it is not specific to cryptocurrencies. You can store almost anything on a Blockchain that you want to have an immutable record of. These could be things such as a will, financial records, mortgage information, property ownership, etc.
- There is no central authority. Blockchain is distributed. This means that there is no central trust. The Blockchain itself provides the trust and the transaction validation mechanisms enforce this trust.
- There is no middleman in transactions, which improves efficiencies and eliminates or lowers transaction fees. Most financial transactions today use a middleman – buying a car, a house, getting a loan, etc. Blockchain eliminates that requirement. Of course, middlemen are still useful for their domain skills. Blockchain does not eliminate that.
- Blockchain is open and transparent. All transactions can be seen, tracked, and even validated by anyone. This means that powerful audit trails are inherent in the technology.

Blockchain was originally devised in 1991 and was intended to time-stamp digital documents.[xcv] The inventors wanted to create a system where digital documents could not be tampered with. In 2009, *Satoshi Nakamoto* adopted Blockchain for use within Bitcoin. Satoshi Nakamoto is a pseudonym. As of this writing no one knows who, or what, Satoshi Nakamoto is. Satoshi Nakamoto released a whitepaper entitled "Bitcoin: A Peer-to-Peer Electronic Cash System."[xcvi] In this paper Satoshi describes the use of a "chain" to secure electronic transactions. Since the release of that paper, numerous individuals and organizations have created different Blockchain offerings. As of late 2018, there are approximately 20 different Blockchain platforms being developed, some derivatives of others.[xcvii]

Hoping to tap into some of the early success of Bitcoin, thousands of new cryptocurrencies have been created, with a market cap well over $200 billion.[xcviii] Like any currency, cryptocurrencies need exchanges to trade on. There are now more than 500 cryptocurrency exchanges.[xcix]

Blockchain is designed to be inherently secure, although recently some vulnerabilities have been surfacing[c]. Time will tell if it's as secure as anticipated.

In Blockchain, data is stored in blocks (files containing data such as Bitcoin transactions). The data in each block is hashed, and that hash is stored in

the block. A hash is a *fingerprint* of the data. If you change the da
the hash. There are a number of hashing algorithms and one of t
lar ones is SHA-256.[ci] SHA stands for Secure Hashing Algorithm
refers to how many bits are used in the calculation. Bitcoin us
its cryptography.[cii]

What makes SHA-256 (and other hashing algorithms) incredibly secure is that it is one way. In other words, passing a string of characters though a hashing function generates a unique string of characters that cannot be examined to determine the original value. Said more simply, when you hash a string, the resulting string cannot be used to determine what the original string was.

Hashing also ensures that changing even a small element of the original string results in a completely different hash.

Consider the phrase "The Internet of Intelligent Things." When passed through a SHA-256 hashing function, it generates the following string of characters:

4252102A5C74D0FE5CFDC62CF0C6A1318A6B1373D010365C1D-F6B4313E459C60

If we change just one letter in the phrase (let's change the "o" in "of" to an uppercase "O") so we now have "The Internet Of Intelligent Things." Passing this new phrase to the SHA-256 hashing function, we now get:

AF1092E73C6CACE7A1D9CDE75F15A64C3D5518D-F9653D1AD404562936AF23710

As you can see, even the tiniest changes result in a very different hash. This is one of the features that makes Blockchain so secure. The data in each block is hashed and changing the data changes the hash. There is no computationally efficient way to take that string and turn in back into the original phrase. Note that hashing is not encryption, so there is no way to *decrypt* a hash.

You can try this for yourself. Simply search on the Internet for "SHA256 Hash Generator" and you will find a number of online sites that offer this capability. Enter slightly different strings and notice how the resulting has is quite different, even with small changes.

Have you ever wondered how a website or service remembers and validates your password? A good website will never store your password in plain text, instead they will store a hashed copy of your password. When you type in your password to gain access, they will hash that password and compare the hash with the hashed password you used when you first set up your ount. That way, if ever the site was compromised, a hacker only gets access to your hashed password and not the actual one. Of course, this assumes that the website is following appropriate security protocols, and not all do. In early 2018, 773 million consumer accounts had their email and passwords exposed across multiple websites.[ciii] Even if you use strong passwords, it's a good habit to change them periodically. Actually, it's a very good habit to change them periodically.

I mentioned earlier that the data in each block in Blockchain is hashed, and that hash is stored in the block. But that alone is not enough to make the Blockchain secure. In the Blockchain, each block also has the hash of the previous block. This prevents tampering as you would have to change the hash of every single block in the Blockchain even if you changed a single character. And, because Blockchain is distributed, each Blockchain node has a complete copy of the Blockchain, so you'd also have to change the Blockchains of thousands of other nodes.[civ] This would be computationally impossible and an attempt to do so would be quickly caught by the other nodes on the network. Blockchain is primarily secure due to the astronomical amount of computing effort it would take to compromise it.

There is an attack known as the 51 percent attack which means that an attacker would have to gain control of at least 51% of the Blockchain to compromise it.[cv] As a Blockchain grows this attack becomes increasingly difficult to achieve, but there have been recent examples.[cvi]

Before data is written to the Blockchain, the transaction is verified by other nodes on the network. This is known as consensus.[cvii] In other words, other nodes come to consensus (a general agreement) that the transaction is legitimate before it is allowed to be written. There are a number of consensus algorithms and one of the more popular ones is known as Proof of Work.[cviii] Proof of Work is used to confirm transactions and add new blocks to the chain. Computers in the Blockchain network compete against each other by performing mathematical calculations. Those that complete the calculations the quickest get rewarded via the payment of small amounts of cryptocurrency. This is also known as mining.

Mining is the process by which transactions are verified and added to the Blockchain. The mining process involves compiling recent transactions into blocks and trying to solve a computationally difficult puzzle. In the early days of Bitcoin and Blockchain, mining was quite profitable for some and some made significant amounts of money. Today, due to the increasingly complex algorithms used, Bitcoin mining is not nearly as profitable as it once was due to the massive amounts of computing equipment and energy needed to perform the mining calculations.

Proof of Work (mining) has several limitations. It is very time consuming. Professional minors may invest millions of dollars into dedicated mining hardware in an attempt to get an edge up on the competition. Specialized hardware containing ASICs (application-specific integrated circuit—a chip designed for mining rather than general use) are now typically used as they can mine much faster than off the shelf hardware.[cix]

Mining also consumes a great deal of energy. Miners need a high amount of computing power in order to find the solution, which leads to a significant use of energy and money. It is estimated that Bitcoin consumed 7.7 gigawatts by the end of 2018 – that's almost three times the energy consumed by the country of Ireland.[cx] Environmental issues aside, when Bitcoin prices were high, it made more financial sense to spend the money on energy to mine Bitcoin, but now it's not financially viable for most.

Proof of work (mining) is not the only consensus mechanism. There are several others all with their own pros and cons[cxi]. For example, another consensus mechanism is known as Proof of Stake.[cxii] In this model, the block creator (also known as the validator) is chosen based on their wealth. They can mine or validate blocks based on how much Bitcoin (for example) they own. In this system the miners are called forgers. The more coins someone has in this model, the more mining power they hold.

As Proof of Work becomes unsustainable due to costs (energy and computation), it is likely that we'll see more and more efficient methods adopted. If Bitcoin proves to be a long-term sustainable electronic currency, it will likely evolve to take advantage of some of these more energy-efficient methods.

In addition to being highly secure, as we've seen, the data in Blockchain is also immutable – meaning it cannot be changed. Because the data cannot be changed, if it comes from a trusted source, it could be argued that it can be trusted. This removes the need for intermediary trusted parties and allows transactions to occur much more rapidly than they might otherwise.

Consider for example, the scenario of sending some money to your friend. Today, you might first send your money to a trusted party like your bank or PayPal, and they would forward the money on to your friend. This takes time however, often a few days. They have to verify that your friend is who they say they are, that you have the funds you claim, etc. They likely also take a small percentage of the transaction as a transaction fee. With Blockchain this scenario changes significantly. Now, you simply send your friend the money, and the platform does all these checks for you, often in a matter of minutes. There is no middleman, no fees are taken out, and it takes considerably less time. It's easy to see why Blockchain is attracting a lot of attention.

There are currently three types of Blockchain networks: Public Blockchains, Private Blockchains, and Consortium Blockchains.

Public Blockchains are just that, they are public. There are no access restrictions. Anyone with an internet connection and a computer can post transactions as well as become a validator of transactions (participate in mining). Some of the largest, most known public Blockchains are Bitcoin and Ethereum (another type of cryptocurrency).

A Private Blockchain is a permissioned Blockchain, meaning that you need permission to join it before you can access it. One cannot join a permissioned Blockchain unless they are invited by the administrator. These types of Blockchains may be used by companies who want to use the technology but are not comfortable using a public Blockchain such as the one Bitcoin uses.

Finally, Consortium Blockchains are private but consist of specific, invited, organizations sharing the same Blockchain. This might be used where multiple companies do business with one another but do not want to use a public Blockchain. For example, a group of companies involved in a supply chain (the sequence of processes involved in the production and distribution of something such as food or parts) may all be part of a consortium Blockchain. These companies might like to track the location and condition of the product using a private Blockchain so that each company in the process has visibility, but without sharing the details publicly.

The security, immutability of data, faster transactions, and reduced cost make Blockchain attractive for cryptocurrencies, but the applications beyond cryptocurrencies are profound. There are potentially numerous applications for the Internet of Intelligent Things such as micro-transactions between things, or enhanced security of connected devices.

As we discussed earlier, IoT devices can be compromised due to lack of authentication and security models. Blockchain could potentially address this.

Let's say you buy an IoT device online, how do you know it hasn't been tampered with? How do you know it doesn't contain malware (software designed to damage, or gain unauthorized access to a computer)? How do you know it has the latest security patches installed? Generally speaking, you don't. With Blockchain however, you could validate the device details against information a trusted manufacturer placed onto Blockchain about that device.

Think of it this way. Your IoT device runs software. Software is nothing more than a string of characters executed by the device. Just as we performed a hash of a string earlier, it's trivial for a computer to calculate the hash of the software on a device.

If the manufacturer stored the hash of the software intended to run on the device, on the Blockchain, your network could compare the hash of what's on your device against what the manufacturer says it should be, and you'd authoritatively know if the device had been compromised.

In addition to the software running on the device, Blockchain could be used to allow IoT devices to securely exchange data between them, establishing trust. Just like people exchanging money, devices could exchange data in the same trusted way. Would you trust your connected camera to allow your connected door lock to unlock your front door? Today that might be questionable, but with an immutable, secure relationship between them, enabled by Blockchain, you might feel more comfortable. The benefits are more apparent when numerous IoT devices are transacting with one another across homes, cities, or event countries.

It is worth mentioning one last feature of Blockchain supported by some implementations, and that feature is known as Smart Contracts.[cxiii]

Smart Contracts are basically programs (code) that reside on the Blockchain. Like all other data on the Blockchain, they are immutable. Once written to the Blockchain, they cannot be changed. Newer versions can be added, but they would negate the previous version. There are number of programming languages used to create Smart Contracts, and one of the more popular ones is known as Solidity[cxiv]. Solidity is used on the Ethereum Blockchain.

Smart Contracts can be executed automatically when a given event occurs. Let's say you owned a Blockchain-enabled car in the future. Once you charged your car, your car could automatically inform a Smart Contract to pay the bill for the electricity consumed. A Smart Contract could automatically pay a shipper when a package arrived safely. It could also update the distributed ledger (Blockchain) to create an immutable record of the delivery.

With billions of IoT devices on the Internet, Blockchain-enabled IoT devices could be transformative. Devices could have sophisticated rules that automatically execute when conditions are met. Smart homes become *intelligent* homes. A smart thermostat might communicate energy usage to a smart grid when a certain number of wattage hours had been reached. A smart contract could then automatically transfer money from your account to the electric company, while also passing along energy usage, effectively automating the meter reader and the billing process.

Autonomous vehicles could *talk* to one another on the roads warning one another of dangers ahead, or traffic congestion. Appliances could automatically order replacement parts while knowing that the replacement parts were not counterfeit.

The possibilities are endless.

It is still early days for Blockchain, but the coupling of IoT and technologies like Blockchain could allow for an entirely different, secure and trusted, connected world providing the benefits IoT promises without the compromise of security and privacy. IoT and Smart Contracts give us a distributed intelligence on a scale never seen before, not just an Internet of Things, but an Internet of secure, Intelligent Things.

9. POWER IN NUMBERS

"There is always strength in numbers."
- Mark Stephen Shields, American political columnist and commentator.

In 2012 I wrote a small piece called "Internet of Everything: A drop of water",[cxv] where I stated that "A single drop by itself is not that significant. Yet, when combined with millions or even billions of other drops, it can change the face of our planet." Billions of things working together can make a difference. A single thing connected to the Internet has limited value, but when billions of things are connected, that value is multiplied exponentially.

It's not one thing that's going to be the next "big thing," it's billions of things working together that will create amazing new experiences.

There have been many projections attempting to calculate how many things will be connected to the Internet by given date. In 2011, I myself projected that there would be 50 billion things connected to the Internet by 2020. I was not the only one. A year earlier, Ericsson's former CEO Hans Vestburg was among the first to state it in a 2010 presentation to shareholders. There have even been some fantastical projections of 1 trillion things[cxvi] in the next few years. I'm very skeptical of that projection, as the math does not hold up. I think we are a long way from a trillion things on the Internet, but it could happen, eventually.

Some have asked how I came up with my 50 billion number. I had the good fortune of working for Cisco for 24 years, from 1990 to 2014, and I kept track of Internet growth statistics while I was there, for presentations I gave and articles I wrote. I tracked how many users were connected over the course of 20 years, looked at the average growth by year and extrapolated forward to 2020. I was relatively conservative in my estimate and did not account for unknown or yet to be invented things.

As often happens, reality has not quite matched the hype, and a few years ago I revised my estimates to be around 30 billion things by 2020, which seems to be in line with the general consensus.[cxvii] Over the last few years, different companies have put forth their estimates[cxviii], and if we average them all out, it comes to about 28 billion things by 2020.

2014 EMC – 32 billion by 2020

2015 Gartner – 20.8 billion by 2020

2015 IDC – 30 billion by 2020

2016 Juniper – 46 billion by 2021

2016 Cisco – 26.3 billion by 2020

2016 Ericsson – 28 billion by 2021

2017 Gartner – 20.4 billion by 2020

2017 Business Insider – 22.5 billion by 2021

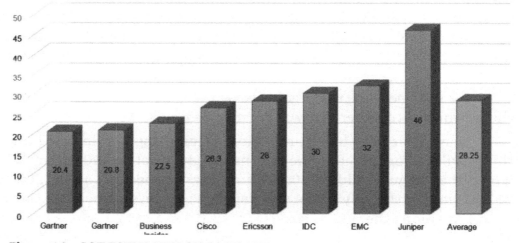

Figure 10 – IOT ESTIMATES BY COMPANY

2020 estimates aside, one thing that is stunning about the Internet of Things is how quickly new things are being added.

Let's do a quick thought exercise. If we make the conservative assumptions that there were 10 billion things connected to the Internet in 2015 (some sources are considerably higher[cxix]), and there will be 28 billion by 2020, this means an incremental growth of 18 billion things over the five year span.

There are 31,536,000 seconds in one year (not counting leap years), which means there are 157,680,000 seconds in five years. Those 18 billion new things divided by 157 million seconds suggest that we added about 114 new things every second during that timeframe, on average.

Let's say it takes you about six hours to read this book, by the time you finish reading, about two and a half million new things will have been added to the Internet.

That is staggering growth!

There are a few flaws with this thought exercise. Device growth has fluctuated over the five-year period and people read at different speeds, but the general notion holds true. We are connecting things to the Internet at a blistering rate.

As the world becomes more connected, things that are not connected will be at a growing disadvantage. Eventually, we will look back at this time and be amused at how few things were connected.

A single termite is inconsequential, yet millions of them working together build structures that rival what humans can build.

A single atom is invisible to the naked eye, yet billions of them create life.

A single star barely lights up its corner of the galaxy, yet billions of stars create endless worlds.

The human brain is comprised of billions of neurons, about 86 billion more precisely[cxx], and while a single neuron is not very powerful, billions of them connected together give us consciousness.

IoT shares these same traits.

As we will learn later in the book, artificial intelligence also shares this same trait. Much like the human brain is comprised of billions of neurons, artificial intelligence models are comprised of millions of artificial neurons, and soon may rival that of the human brain.[cxxi]

As IoT and AI converge, there is great power in numbers. This intersection of billions of connected devices coupled with billions of artificial neurons will transform our world.

59

10. HOW IOT WILL CHANGE EVERYTHING

"There is nothing permanent except change."
- Heraclitus. Greek - Philosopher 544 BC - 483 BC

While the numbers behind IoT are staggering, it's the application of IoT that's really important.

According to IDC (International Data Corporation), "by 2025, an average connected person anywhere in the world will interact with connected devices nearly 4,800 times per day - basically one interaction every 18 seconds."[cxxii] The Internet of Things is going to be everywhere.

This type of growth would have been impossible just a few short years ago. A perfect storm of technological forces (which we'll discuss in an upcoming chapter) has allowed us to connect things at an amazing rate.

We are in a period of rational experimentation with IoT. We are testing new business models and consumer acceptance. Some models will survive a long time, whereas others will die off quickly. There are many gimmicky connected devices today and technology has its own "Darwinism." If a device does not serve a useful purpose it will eventually find itself in the technology "junk drawer." Technology for technology's sake is not sustainable.

There are numerous examples of how IoT is impacting every industry. In the consumer space, IoT has a strong foothold in the connected home. Thermostats, lights, smart plugs, security systems, appliances, and automobiles are just a few of the more developed solutions being used.

In healthcare, wearables provide visibility into a person's activities, but this is just the beginning. Healthcare organizations use IoT for remote patient care. This allows patients to receive care at home where they're most comfortable. With wearable sensors, doctors can remotely track and respond to a patients' health status in real time.

Some companies have even taken this a step further with connected pills. One such example is Proteus Digital Health. Proteus Discover is a "digital medicine." It allows health organizations to prescribe a small pill that patients swallow. This ingestible is about the size of a grain of sand. It is attached to the medication that the patient swallows. Once the pill reaches the patient's stomach, it is activated by the stomach acid and transmits to a small patch worn on the body of the patient. This in turn is then transmitted to the Proteus cloud where, with the patient's permission, healthcare providers and caregivers can access the information via a portal. This allows healthcare providers and caregivers to verify whether or not the patient has taken the pill they are supposed to take. In addition, the patch also measures patient activity and rest which can also be shared via the patient portal. The ability to track whether or not a patient has taken a prescribed pill is important, as more than 50% of prescribed medications are not taken as directed.[cxxiii]

Medical assets are often high-value and are not often in abundant supply. When one of these assets is needed, it is often needed quite rapidly. For example, a physician would rather not spend time trying to locate a defibrillator but would rather spend that time trying to help a patient. IoT technology can help monitor and track these medical assets. This allows the staff to spend less time searching and more time spent with patients. The same technology can be used to track patients, medications, and other medical devices as needed.

In industries such as manufacturing, a more robust version of IoT, known as the Industrial Internet of things (IIoT[cxxiv]) is changing the way that industries work. General Electric is credited with coining the term the Industrial Internet in late 2012. They estimated that the Industrial Internet could be a $225 billion market by 2020.[cxxv]

The industrial Internet of Things, also known simply as the Industrial Internet, brings together machines, advanced analytics, and people to help make industries more efficient.

While there isn't always a clear delineation or definition between the Internet of Things and the Industrial Internet of Things, the Internet of Things tends to focus on consumer-type devices such as smart home devices, whereas the Industrial Internet tends to focus on connecting devices and machines in industries such as energy, and manufacturing where there is more at stake, or where system failures and unplanned downtime can result in high risk, or even life-threatening, situations. The Industrial Internet of Things tends to focus on proactive detection, such as determining if a machine is about to fail, or a pipe is about to burst, whereas the Internet of Things tends to focus more on functionality and convenience.

While not completely accurate (as technologies tend to bleed from one industry to the home and vice-versa), the simplest way to think about the differences between the two is that IoT is for the consumer, and IIoT is for industry.

In addition to homes, hospitals, and factories, IoT found its way into the field. One of the first examples I gave in this book was about a Dutch company called Sparked that was connecting sensors to livestock to track their health. This technology has come a long way. Now farmers and growers are using the Internet of Things to grow crops and raise livestock. Sensors in the fields can tell the farmers if the crops need more water, more pesticides, or even if they are being attacked by pests. Sensors on livestock can help farmers monitor the location and health of the animals. One such company called Moocall[cxxvi] helps farmers monitor pregnant cows. A battery-powered sensor detects motion that is associated with oncoming labor. It then sends a text notification via the device's GSM (Global System for Mobile) radio to the farmer.[cxxvii] The farmer can then act accordingly.

Another company called Cropx[cxxviii] uses data and sensor devices to help farmers better understand water usage across their fields. This technology can inform farmers about the amount of fertilizer and pesticides they need.

It will not be long until most fields utilize completely autonomous tractors. Already companies such as John Deere are working on tractors that drive automatically.[cxxix] These tractors can be highly accurate when working rows of crops. They have the ability to avoid reworking the same rows in the field by reducing overlap to less than an inch.[cxxx] This results in farmers saving time and money. This IoT-enabled farming is known in the industry as Precision Ag Technology.[cxxxi]

From our homes to our factories, our hospitals and our fields, you would be hard-pressed to find an industry that is not somehow being reshaped by the Internet of Things. There are countless examples of how IoT is redefining how we work, and ultimately how we live.

But while IoT is changing everything, something is missing. IoT devices are *dumb*. They don't adapt automatically to changing conditions, they lack *intelligence*.

Take the smart home for example. Your connected lights do not turn off automatically to save energy, your connected thermostat will happily continue to heat your home even if the windows are open, your connected sprinkler system will continue to water your lawn even if there is a broken sprinkler head, and your connected oven will happily burn your dinner if left unattended.

Of course, there are exceptions to all of these, but my main point is that for all the amazing things these connected devices do for us, they require more and more care and feeding on our part.

We work more for technology than we have every done before.

Granted, there are several solutions on the market that allow consumers to program their connected devices, to *act* more intelligently, but it's an act.

Therein lies the difference between a smart home, and an *intelligent* home. A smart home is one that is full of connected devices that you can *program* to do things at appropriate times. An intelligent home on the other hand needs no *programming*. The devices learn about you, your habits, and automatically adjust to your needs. No *programming* needed.

I submit that things are about to change in a big way with IoT. In order for a thing, whether it be a human, an animal, or a piece of technology to make a decision, it needs data. As we'll see in the next chapter, we are creating a lot of data. As it turns out, this data is just what IoT devices need to become intelligent.

11. THE ZETTAFLOOD IS COMING

"Data is a precious thing and will last longer than the systems themselves."
- Tim Berners-Lee, inventor of the World Wide Web.

The billions of things connected to the Internet generate massive amounts of data.

The first Apple iPhone which debuted on June 29th, 2007 had a camera sensor capable of taking 2-megapixel images. This is an image that is 1600 pixels wide and 1200 pixels tall. Depending on the compression used, this is approximately a 4 MB file.

The iPhone X / XS currently has a camera sensor capable of taking 12-megapixel images. This is an image that is 4000 pixels wide and 3000 pixels tall. Depending on the compression used, this is approximately a 24 MB file.

In 10 generations of phones, the iPhone has seen a raw pixel improvement of six-fold, and a six-fold requirement for storage per image.

These numbers are fairly insignificant when considering a single photo, or even a single user taking lots of photos, but collectively, we are taking a lot of photos. Consider that in 2017, we took 1.2 trillion new photos.[cxxxii] That's over 180 photos for every person on the planet! Approximately 80% of the photos we take are taken via our mobile phones.[cxxxiii] By 2018, we will be storing more than 5 trillion photos.[cxxxiv]

It's easy to see why. Before digital cameras, not everyone had a film camera. Perhaps a family owned a camera, but today virtually everyone owns a mobile phone with a camera in it. Before digital cameras we were very judicious in how many photos we took. This was because taking pictures relied on film, and a roll of film could only hold so many pictures, and of course there was the hassle of having your film processed. Today we think nothing of taking hundreds, even thousands of pictures while on a trip. Storage space is relatively cheap and abundant.

While we take trillions of photos, video traffic dwarfs all other types of traffic. Cisco's VNI (Visual Networking Index) which forecasts Internet-related growth has some startling projections[cxxxv]:

- "It would take an individual more than 5 million years to watch the amount of video that will cross global IP networks each month in 2021. Every second, a million minutes of video content will cross the network by 2021."
- "Globally, IP video traffic will be 82 percent of all consumer Internet traffic by 2021, up from 73 percent in 2016."
- All of this has huge implications for network traffic. The same index reports:
- "Annual global IP traffic will reach 3.3 Zettabytes by 2021."
- "Global IP traffic will increase nearly threefold over the next 5 years and will have increased 127-fold from 2005 to 2021."

There are many more incredible projections in the report. I encourage you to take a deeper look at their forecasts if this type of material interests you.

As data grows, so does our usage of new terms such as exabytes and zettabytes. These words may not be familiar to all yet, so let me take a moment to put them in perspective.

A single character such as the letter "A" or the number "7" takes up 1 *byte* (a unit of digital information) when stored or transmitted by a computer, assuming no compression used.

An exabyte is 10^{18} bytes, or, in long form, it's 1,000,000,000,000,000,000 bytes[cxxxvi].

A zettabyte is 10^{21} or, in long form, it's 1,000,000,000,000,000,000,000 bytes.

There are 1,000 exabytes in 1 zettabyte.

It is estimated that if you took all the words humans have ever spoken, ever, it would add up to about 5 exabytes. This means that 1 zettabyte is equivalent to 200 times all the words humans have ever spoken.

Now re-read Cisco's forecast: "*Annual global IP traffic will reach 3.3 Zettabytes by 2021.*"

The bottom line here is that by 2021, it is estimated that the global Internet traffic (global IP traffic) will be 660 times all the words humans have <u>ever</u> spoken. The following year it will be significantly more. Let that sink in for a minute.

It should also be noted too that our data is getting *fatter*. Image resolutions are getting higher. 4K televisions are mainstream, yet 8K is just around the corner. New forms of rich media such as virtual reality and augmented reality will continue to push network limits.

There is a caution buried underneath all this data however, and that is that data in itself is not information. There is a hierarchy to data.

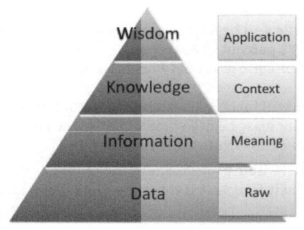

Figure 11 - THE VALUE HIERARCHY OF DATA

Data is the raw material we create, but by itself may not have any specific meaning. If I gave you a number, say 72, without any context it would be meaningless. Does it mean the temperature, someone's age, days until an event, parts per million? It's just data. Data can be analyzed and turned into information, increasing its value. Sufficient information can provide you with knowledge, and enough knowledge can lead to wisdom, or the application of knowledge.

As the data deluge continues, it will become harder to know what data to trust, and ever more difficult to extract the information needed from that data.

Consider an album of digital photos on a personal computer. Say it contained a mere 10 pictures. Finding a single one photo would be easy. Now imagine it contained a thousand photos, a million photos, or more. The time spent looking for something increases proportionally, the storage needed increases, and the technology resources required increases dramatically.

In 2008, the World created about five exabytes of new data, at least according to Eric Schmidt, the chairman and previous CEO of Google.[cxxxvii]

That means that we created more new data in one year that we did in all of human history[cxxxviii]. Just a few years later, in 2011, we were creating about 1.2 zettabytes of data – that's equivalent to about 20 billion fully-loaded 64GB Apple iPads. By some estimates we will be generating 100 zettabytes of new data annually by 2025.[cxxxix] That's equivalent to 36 billion years of high-definition video.

IDC forecasts that it may be even higher. By 2025 they forecast that the global datasphere will grow to 163 zettabytes.[cxl] That's ten times the 16.1 zettabytes generated only a decade earlier in 2016.

The numbers may prove to be accurate or overblown, but the fact remains that we are creating a lot of data. So much so that the industry has adopted the term Big Data[cxli] to define the voluminous amount of data we are creating.

Video is arguably the largest contributor when it comes to data. By 2022 video will account for around 75% of mobile data traffic alone.[cxlii]

YouTube, the popular video sharing site publishes its statistics on video uploads – the number of videos that users upload for others to watch. I started tracking this incredible statistic about a decade ago. At that time 48 hours of video were uploaded to YouTube every minute. Two days of video every single minute, and it has been steadily growing since then. As of May 2019, approximately 500 hours of video were uploaded to YouTube every minute.[cxliii] To put that in perspective, that's 30,000 years of video uploaded to YouTube annually. You would need 400 lifetimes to watch it all!

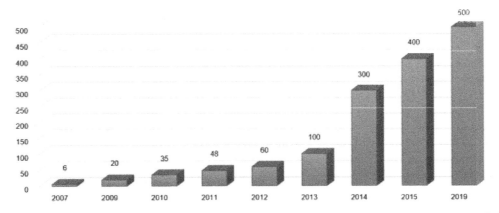

Figure 12 - HOURS OF YOUTUBE VIDEO UPLOADED EVERY MINUTE. DATA SOURCE: YOUTUBE.

We are now creating more new data every 10 minutes than we did in all of human history, and remarkably, by some estimates, we store 92% of all this data we come across.[cxliv]

At this point you might be thinking, "what could we possibly do with all of this data?" As humans, it's overwhelming. But for machines, all of this data is wonderful fodder for machine learning. Unfortunately, it also comes with some significant dangers.

12. THE DARK SIDE OF BIG DATA

"**Big Brother is Watching You.**"

- George Orwell's *1984*

We are creating more new data in minutes than we did in entire decades previously. Data, like many things is just a tool. How we choose to the use tool matters. Data can be used to enlighten, and it can be used to control. It is difficult to discuss a dystopian future without the mention of George Orwell's defining novel *1984*.[cxlv] Published in 1949, *1984* imagines a dystopian vision of a totalitarian, bureaucratic world.

It ranks among the most terrifying novels ever written.[cxlvi]

The book touches on the invasion of privacy and ubiquitous surveillance. Could such a world exist, or is it purely science fiction?

As we now know, this is all enabled by big data.

In mid-2013 it was publicized that the United States National Security Agency (NSA) had been secretly monitoring and storing global internet traffic, including the bulk data collection of email and phone call data.

From the NSA's web site: "The National Security Agency/Central Security Service (NSA/CSS) leads the U.S. Government in cryptology that encompasses both signals intelligence (SIGINT) and information assurance (now referred to as cybersecurity) products and services, and enables computer network operations (CNO) in order to gain a decision advantage for the Nation and our allies under all circumstances."[cxlvii]

As this news was made public, sales of the book, *1984*, increased by up to seven times within the first week of 2013.[cxlviii] It was no coincidence. People were concerned, and they should be.

In the book, there are some distinct themes that Orwell discusses, and their relevance to today is perhaps even more significant that it was in the

year 1984.
- Orwell talks about the **ubiquity of television** as a means to control the masses, to feed them information. Televisions are nothing more than a means to access and view information. We now have this capability in everyone's hands – the Smart Phone.
- He talks about **distortion of the language**. How often have you heard the phrase Fake News in the media? Once a term meant to refer to distorted information, the term itself is now used to distort facts and create personal agendas.
- The citizens in 1984 were under **constant, ubiquitous surveillance**. Consider that the number of CCTV (closed-circuit TV) cameras in London is expected to reach 642,000 by 2020 – about 1 for every 14 people.[cxlix] Many other cities are similar.
- **Mass media** was another theme. Today we know this as social media. On average, a person spends 5 years, 4 months on social media in their lifetime. TV, about 7 years, 8 months. Together, about 12 years of your life is spent on social media and television. Do you think this influences you?
- **Bulk data collection of email and phone call data** was another theme. The NSA looks at more than 29 petabytes of the Internet per day[cl], and they are far from the only government or private entity collecting data on a large scale.

Does all this mean that a world like *1984* is inevitable? No, but it's a slippery slope, one we have already lost some footing on. Once your personal data is given away, it's very difficult, if not impossible in many cases, to get it back.

Freedom House is a pro-democracy think tank. On their website, they discuss "The Rise of Digital Authoritarianism" and how "governments around the world are tightening control over citizens' data and using claims of "fake news" to suppress dissent, eroding trust in the internet as well as the foundations of democracy."

In 2018, they released a sobering report.[cli] In it they state that "governments in 18 countries increased state surveillance between June 2017 and now, with 15 considering new "data protection" laws, which can require companies to store user data locally and potentially make it easier for governments to access."[clii] In addition, the report goes on to say, "governments in 32 countries used paid commentators, bots, and trolls in an effort to manipulate online conversations." And, "in the United States, internet freedom declined in 2018 due to the Federal Communications Commission's repeal of net neutrality rules. Other countries fared much worse — 17 out of 65 surveyed had adopted laws restricting online media." There was also mention of cutting off Internet services in an attempt to control the flow of information between citizens.

The trend is concerning. Some key findings in the report state:

- "Declines outnumber gains for the eighth consecutive year. Out of the 65 countries assessed in Freedom on the Net, 26 experienced a deterioration in internet freedom."
- "Authorities demand control over personal data: Governments in 18 countries increased surveillance, often eschewing independent oversight and weakening encryption in order to gain unfettered access to data."

This is disturbing and begs the question, what happens when this data is used not only to influence behavior but also to punish those who don't conform? Concerningly, history is witnessing a real-world example happening in China.

Similar to the FICO credit score in the US, China's social credit score (SCS) amasses information about past transactions and interactions. It then ranks individuals based on their trustworthiness. While this social credit score includes financial information, it moves far beyond simple financial transactions. It is important to note, that at this time, the SCS is voluntary. Citizens opt-in.

In 2018, The Conversation, a network of not-for-profit media outlets that publish news stories written by academics and researchers,[cliii] published an article that stated: "with a mission to 'raise the awareness of integrity and the level of trustworthiness of Chinese society'[cliv], the Chinese government is planning to roll out the system to 1.4 billion citizens, and to make the system fully operational by 2020."[clv] While aspects of the system have been implemented, as of this writing the system is not yet fully implemented, due to the sheer size of the effort as well it being "bureaucratically challenging."[clvi]

The company overseeing this program is Sesame Credit. Sesame Credit, also known as Zhima Credit, is a private credit scoring and loyalty program system developed by Ant Financial Services Group (AFSG), an affiliate of the Chinese Alibaba Group.[clvii]

To build a better sense of someone's overall moral character, the data is classified into five categories. This is turn is used to rate participants:

1. Credit History. Does the person pay their bills on time?
2. Fulfillment Capacity. Is a person able to fulfill their contract

obligations?
3. Personal Characteristics. Is a person's information (like phone number or address) verifiable and accurate?
4. Behavior and Preferences. Is a person's online behavior (shopping for example) desirable?
5. Interpersonal Relationships. Does a person surround themselves with good people? What are the characteristics of their friends?

Actions that might appear mundane by many standards are now used to affect one's social credit. Things like cheating on an online game, smoking in a restricted area, leaving a false product review, not cancelling a reservation to a restaurant you can no longer make, or even jaywalking – all are actions that could affect your social credit score. And because interpersonal relationships are factored in as well, even if a person avoids "negative" behaviors they could still be punished if their friends or family engage in them, so there is an incentive to avoid those deemed undesirable.

Doing good deeds can increase your score and garner rewards. For example, performing charity work, giving blood, cleaning up garbage, or recycling. Citizens are then rewarded with benefits such as shorter wait times, cheaper public transportation, etc. Those with low scores however may receive punishments such as restricted travel.

Most cities participating in this system in China use a points system. Citizens start off with 100 points and can gain or lose points via actions described earlier.

Xi Jinping, a Chinese politician serving as general secretary of the Communist Party of China (CPC) describes the system's foundation as "Once untrustworthy, always restricted."[clviii]

These types of programs are not unique to China, though the scale of the Chinese program is currently unmatched. In October of 2018, the United States Transportation Security Administration (TSA) announced their facial recognition roadmap.[clix] "The program will start by teaming with Customs and Border Protection on biometric security for international travel, followed by putting the technology into use for TSA Precheck travelers to speed up the boarding process. After that, it would both devise an 'opt-in' biometric system for ordinary domestic passengers and flesh out a deeper infrastructure."

While the TSA claims that they hope to reduce the need for physical forms of identification, face recognition is not without its challenges.

According to an article in UK's The Independent, "Facial recognition software used by the UK's biggest police force has returned false positives in more than 98 per cent of alerts generated."[clx]

A freedom of information request showed that the Metropolitan Police's system produced 104 alerts of which only two were later confirmed to be positive matches. The same system used by another police force, the South Wales Police, "returned more than 2,400 false positives in 15 deployments since June 2017." Fewer than 10 percent were correct matches. Both forces were trialing the software and while face recognition systems might be fine for protecting the contents of your smart phone, the technology is suspect when used with large crowds.

The use of Big Data is not unique to governments. Many private companies rely on big data as a business model. Some of these companies run into trouble though their handling of user data. A recent example in the news concerns Facebook, a very popular social media site, and Cambridge Analytica, a British political consulting firm that specializes in what it calls 'behavioral microtargeting'.

In 2014, a researcher named Alexander Kogan (a Russian American who worked at the University of Cambridge) created a personality quiz (a Facebook app called "This Is Your Digital Life") that 270,000 Facebook users would go on to install. From those downloads alone, he was able to harvest the personal information of up to 87 million people, according to Facebook's 2018 estimate.[clxi] It not only collected data from people who took the quiz, but it also exposed a loophole in a Facebook API that allowed it to collect data from the Facebook friends of the quiz takers as well. He then passed that data along to Cambridge Analytica, which would use it to target voters in the 2016 presidential election.

In 2019, Facebook was fined $5 billion as a result of the Cambridge Analytica scandal as well as other privacy breaches.[clxii]

The use of Big Data by governments and private corporations is clearly growing, but there are efforts to strike a better balance. In May of 2018, the European Union passed a regulation called The General Data Protection Regulation 2016/679 (GDPR).[clxiii] GDPR requires businesses to protect the personal data and privacy of EU citizens for transactions that occur within EU member states. GDPR provides protection for the following types of individual's data:[clxiv]

- Basic identity information such as name, address, and ID numbers
- Web data such as location, IP address, cookie data and RFID tags
- Health and genetic data

- Biometric data
- Racial or ethnic data
- Political opinions
- Sexual orientation

Non-compliance could cost companies, and even some public agencies[clxv] significantly. The GDPR imposes stiff fines for violations. The following 10 criteria are used to determine the amount of the fine[clxvi]:

1. Nature of infringement: number of people affected, damaged they suffered, duration of infringement, and purpose of processing.
2. Intention: whether the infringement is intentional or negligent.
3. Mitigation: actions taken to mitigate damage to data subjects.
4. Preventative measures: how much technical and organizational preparation the firm had previously implemented to prevent non-compliance.
5. History: Past relevant infringements, which may be interpreted to include infringements under the Data Protection Directive and not just the GDPR, and past administrative corrective actions under the GDPR, from warnings to bans on processing and fines.
6. Cooperation: how cooperative the firm has been with the supervisory authority to remedy the infringement.
7. Data type: what types of data the infringement impacts.
8. Notification: whether the infringement was proactively reported to the supervisory authority by the firm itself or a third party.
9. Certification: whether the firm had qualified under approved certifications or adhered to approved codes of conduct.
10. Other: other aggravating or mitigating factors may include financial impact on the firm from the infringement.

There are different tiers for fines based upon the infringement. At the lower level, "up to €10 million, or 2% of the worldwide annual revenue of the prior financial year, whichever is higher.[clxvii] At the upper level, "up to €20 million, or 4% of the worldwide annual revenue of the prior financial year, whichever is higher."[clxviii]

These are some good incentives for a company to protect your data and your privacy.

GDPR is specific to the EU as of this writing. Time will tell if other countries adopt such regulations.

In addition to governments taking action, industry leaders are taking a stand. Tim Cook, the CEO of Apple recently warned that modern technology has led to the creation of a "data-industrial complex" in which private and everyday information is "weaponized against us with military efficiency." He went on to call for comprehensive US privacy laws.[clxix] He added that this mechanism doesn't just affect individuals, it affects entire societies.

He couldn't be more right.

Tim Berners-Lee, the inventor of the World Wide Web (WWW) is proposing a technological approach to the problem. He argues that "a handful of companies own vast swaths of web activity[clxx]" such as Facebook for social networking, Google for searching, eBay for auctions, etc. Each of these companies has limited competition giving them unprecedented power over their users. This was not the design of the WWW he argues. The goal for the WWW was for decentralized, distributed content, not centralized, and that everyone would have their own home page and could post their own thoughts.

As a result, Tim Berners-Lee has been working on a concept he calls Solid.[clxxi] With Solid, users store their data in *PODS*, or Personal Online Data Stores. PODS are hosted wherever a user likes, but Solid isn't just about storage, it's about permission. Solid lets applications ask for data, that users grant permission to.

Solid has a tough road ahead and will be going against some large players that dominate the industry. But, if anyone has the vision and possibility to tackle the data privacy issue, Tim Berners-Lee brings a wealth of experience to the problem.

Big Data is neither good nor bad – it's just data, and data is just a tool. How we choose to the use tool is what matters. Big data is helping to solve some huge challenges, yet the dystopian trend around the use of big data is growing and needs to be watched and reacted to carefully.

Dystopian concerns aside, the massive proliferation of big data is also creating "attentional bottlenecks", at least according to new research by Professor Thomas T Hills -

Department of Psychology, University of Warwick.[clxxii] In this research Professor Hills looks at the "Dark Side of Information Proliferation."[clxxiii] He discusses the "'information bottleneck we all face', and the 'severe pitfalls' of the psychological processes behind the shortcuts and sifting methods we intuitively employ to try to deal with that increasing torrent of ever evolving information." Because we are forced to deal with too much information, we take shortcuts in how we process the information. One example he discusses is social bias, or "following the herd." Some users can be quick to jump on the information bandwagon because everyone else is, or a celebrity said so, versus doing their own research.

He concludes his paper with "There are well-understood psychological limits on our capacity to process information. The unfortunate reality is that these limits are forcing us down an evolutionary relationship with information that is losing sight of our best interests. People didn't evolve in an information environment anything like the one we currently experience. And the evidence suggests that things are rapidly moving beyond our control.[clxxiv]" With the advent of artificial intelligence (which we'll discuss in detail later), fake news may be too easy to generate and too hard to discern from the truth.[clxxv]

We are embarking upon uncertain times when it comes to trusting the written word.

It's an interesting observation, big data is new to us. Never before in human history have we had to deal with such a deluge of data. It is becoming ever more challenging to separate valid, reliable data from all the *noise*.

But while there is a dark side to big data, it also has a significant benefit—it provides critical information for our emerging *intelligent* machines.

13. UNDERSTANDING AI

"Intelligence is the ability to adapt to change."

- Stephen Hawking, Theoretical physicist

We hear a lot about artificial intelligence in the media, yet it is not generally understood by the masses. Some believe a robot uprising is inevitable, others are simply concerned about losing their jobs to a machine. While there is a lot of hype around artificial intelligence, let's break it down to what it really is.

Simply put, artificial intelligence is intelligence *demonstrated* by machines. Humans and other animals demonstrate *natural* intelligence. In other words, it is innate.

Defining intelligence is not easy and there is no general agreement on what it means to be intelligent.[clxxvi] It has long been the debate of philosophers.[clxxvii] At what point is a living thing considered intelligent. Is a human cell intelligent? What about an amoeba? What about a house fly or a plant?

For our purposes, we'll use the Wikipedia definition[clxxviii] and general qualities we believe a human to possess to be intelligent. These are "the capacity for logic, understanding, self-awareness, learning, emotional knowledge, reasoning, planning, creativity, critical thinking, and problem solving."

It is perhaps easier to define what is not intelligent vs. what is. A brick for example, is not intelligent. And, machines of course are not intelligent, so we give them the illusion of intelligence by creating it artificially.

I say illusion because at this point in human history we do not yet know if we can create truly intelligent machines. At the current state, machines are far from intelligent. They are getting much better at recognizing human language, objects, people, and more. However, at this point, these are just very sophisticated algorithms.

The Oxford dictionary defines an algorithm as "a process or set of rules to be followed in calculations or other problem-solving operations, especially by a computer."

To illustrate, let's say you had an unsorted list of numbers, and you were tasked with finding the largest number in the list. How would you do this? Well, you might use an algorithm to find the largest number. It might look something like this.

1. Take the first number in the list, write it down.
2. Now, go through all the remaining numbers, and compare each number one by one to the first number that you wrote down.
3. If any one of those numbers is larger than the number you wrote down, replace the number you wrote down with this new number.
4. Repeat this process for the rest of the numbers.

This is an example, albeit a cumbersome one, of an algorithm. Of course, computers are much faster than us at these types of tasks, and this would be a trivial task for a computer to perform.

Why is this important? Well, we're all familiar with examples of computers beating humans at certain games. In 1997, the IBM computer Deep Blue beat the world chess champion Garry Kasparov at chess.[clxxix] This was a significant accomplishment for a machine to beat a human grandmaster in a game he had played almost his entire life.

In March 2016, Google's Deep Mind AlphaGo computer beat Lee Sedol, who at the time was the best human Go player in the world.[clxxx] This win earned AlphaGo a 9 dan professional ranking, which is the highest certification in this game.

Go is an ancient Chinese game developed more than 2,500 years ago. It is believed to be the oldest board game still played today.[clxxxi] Go is a strategy board game for two players. The aim is to surround more territory than the opponent. Although the rules are simple, the game is deceptively complex.

The board of Go is a 19x19 grid, for a total of 361 squares. Compare this with a chess board, which has 8x8 squares, or a total of 64 squares:

THE INTERNET OF INTELLIGENT THINGS

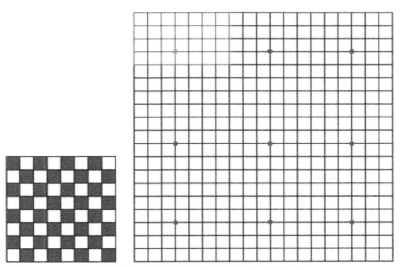

Figure 13 - CHESS VS. GO BOARD COMPARISON

The possible number of first moves in chess is 400 moves (20 white pieces x 20 black pieces). In Go however, there are 32,490 possible first moves.[clxxxii] The estimated number of possible board configuration in chess is 10^{120}. That's the number 10 followed by 120 zeros:

1,000,000,000,000,000,000,000,000,000,000,000,000,000,000,000,000,000,000,000,000,000,000,000,000,000,000,000,000,000,000,000,000,000,000,000,000,000,000,000,000,000,000.

This is a huge number. However, to put this in perspective relative to Go, Go has around 10^{174} possible board combinations, which looks like this:
10,000,000,000,000,000,000,000,000,000,000,000,000,000,000,000,000,000,000,000,000,000,000,000,000,000,000,000,000,000,000,000,000,000,000,000,000,000,000,000,000,000,000,000,000,000,000,000,000,000,000,000,000,000,000,000,000,000,000,000,000,000,000,000,000.

That's one million trillion trillion trillion trillion more configurations than chess.

This starts to give you an idea of how impressive computers are at crunching numbers. In complex games like chess or Go, not only does the computer have to calculate its own moves, both defensive and offensive, it has to do so in a timely manner. It would not be as impressive if a computer took days to calculate a single move. The supercomputers that IBM and Google are using are able to calculate moves in about the same time that a human might.

Ultimately though it's important to keep in mind that no matter how impressive these computing feats might seem; they are still just examples of computers applying algorithms for a specific task. This should not be confused with true intelligence; it is simply using computing power that can execute algorithms much faster and more efficiently than a human could.

Having said that, the engineering and technical prowess used to build AlphaGo should not be dismissed. In 2017, an improved version of AlphaGo known as AlphaGo Zero debuted. This was a significant evolution of the previous technology. Unlike the earlier versions of AlphaGo which learned how to play by using thousands of human played games as training data, AlphaGo Zero learned to play the game all by itself.

Read that again. It learned to play the game by itself.

It did this by using a "machine learning" (which we'll cover in more depth shortly) technique known as Reinforcement Learning (RL)[clxxxiii], where a computer learns through trial-and-error. Said another way, the computer is its own teacher.

It starts off with a neural network (we'll also cover that in more detail later) that knows nothing about the game. It then plays thousands of games against itself and the neural network is tuned and updated. As it plays each iteration of the game the system improves each time. Eventually after many iterations it is able to reach and exceed human level performance. This is an important technique as it requires no human input and therefore is not limited by human knowledge. Over the course of millions of iterations of the game, AlphaGo Zero discovered new knowledge. It developed unconventional strategies and new approaches that masters of the game Go are now studying.

The machine taught *us* something.

To understand in more detail how all of this was accomplished, it is worth taking a few minutes to read the paper on the deep mind website.[clxxxiv]

When we talk about algorithms for artificial intelligence and machine learning, it's the same type of thing, just more complex and a lot more sophisticated. But, when all is said and done, it is simply a machine following a set of steps to compute an output.

Over time as computing devices become ever faster, we may have trouble discerning if a machine is truly intelligent, or simply provides the illusion of intelligence. For many tasks, it simply won't matter.

Humans have had a long history with artificial intelligence. For centuries we have written about and attempted to build intelligent machines. Some of the earliest artificial beings appear in Greek myths.[clxxxv] We have built automatons attempting to replicate human behavior. We have written numerous books, and have produced many movies, containing artificial, intelligent life forms. Characters such as Maria in Fritz Lang's film Metropolis, HAL in the movie 2001 - A Space Odyssey, Data in the Star Trek television series, David in the movie Prometheus, and of course the infamous Terminator to name just a few.

The modern field of artificial intelligence was born at a workshop held on the campus of Dartmouth College during the summer of 1956.[clxxxvi] Interest and efforts in the field have ebbed and flowed over the last few decades but have recently gained a resurgence.

The real value of artificial intelligence, from a technical perspective, is that machines learn without having humans having to write new programs each time. Today we use highly specialized programs. For example, you might use a spreadsheet to work with numbers, a web browser to surf the web, a photo album to manage pictures, and so on. These programs tend to do one thing, and one thing well. You wouldn't surf the web with your spreadsheet program, and you wouldn't use a word processor to perform calculations on numbers. Of course, some applications share some abilities of others, but generally speaking we use one application to perform a specific task. This is what makes artificial intelligence so powerful. You create one program that is very flexible, which can then be used for a variety of scenarios.

A deep discussion on artificial intelligence is outside the scope of this book, and there are many good books on the subject, albeit some quite technical, so I will cover mainly the highlights that are relevant to the topic at hand, the Internet of Intelligent Things.

There are two main branches of artificial intelligence. Applied AI and Generalized AI. Applied AI focuses on carrying out one specific task. Examples are tasks such as image recognition, handwriting recognition, or voice recognition.

Generalized AI, on the other hand, is an attempt to develop machine intelligence that is general purpose. Generalized AI aims to build a machine with intelligence comparable to that of at least the human mind. This is arguably the holy Grail of artificial intelligence.

You may also hear the term "cognitive computing." This is a euphemism for artificial intelligence. Because of how artificial intelligence has been portrayed in books and movies, it has developed a negative connotation. When one thinks of intelligent machines, images such as the Terminator come to mind, so cognitive computing is sometimes used as a less scary term.

As you read more about artificial intelligence, you will quickly run into additional terms such machine learning and deep learning. While the topics themselves can become quite sophisticated, and quite technical, at a high level there is a simply, hierarchical relationship between the three.

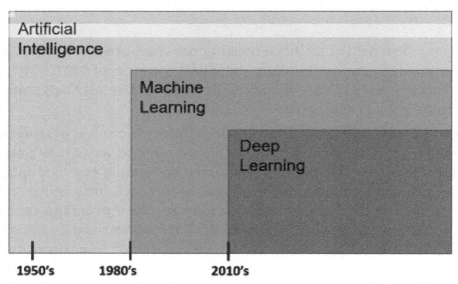

Figure 14 - THE RELATIONSHIP OF AI TO MACHINE LEARNING TO DEEP LEARNING

Artificial intelligence is the broad umbrella term for attempting to make computers think more like humans. It is not specific to any given approach or technique but rather encapsulates the overall field.

Machine learning uses statistical techniques to give machines the ability to learn without being explicitly programed. The term machine learning was coined in 1959 by Arthur Samuel, an American pioneer in the field of computer gaming and artificial intelligence.[clxxxvii]

Within the machine learning category, there is deep learning. It has two sub-categories, supervised learning[clxxxviii] and un-supervised learning.

To understand supervised learning, imagine it's your first day on a new job. Your supervisor sits with you and shows you, in detail, how to do your job. After some time, you show proficiency in the task and the supervisor goes away, and you are able to do the job all by yourself. This is analogous to supervised learning.

In contrast, imagine that it's your first day on a new job, but this time you are all alone. There is no supervisor that sits with you. You have to figure out how to do the job by yourself. There may be some clues, for example the tools on your desk, some old paperwork you found, etc. After a while you finally figure out how to do your job. It takes a lot longer, and you make more mistakes, but eventually you learn how to do your job. This is analogous to unsupervised learning.

While this is an oversimplification of the approaches to machine learning, this should help you understand the general concept.

Now let's go slightly deeper.

With supervised learning the computer is given example inputs (known as the training data) with desired outputs. The goal is for the machine to learn a general rule that maps the inputs to the outputs. The idea behind supervised learning is that you train the machine to recognize something, so next time it encounters it, it recognizes it.

An example of this is handwriting recognition. You might feed the machine, or more accurately an algorithm, with hundreds or thousands of examples of handwriting. These are the example inputs or the training data. Using this training data, you train the algorithm to map given handwriting styles to expected letters of the alphabet, or words. Now that the algorithm has been trained, next time it is presented with unknown handwriting examples it will more accurately recognize the handwriting.

You may have already used this technique and not realized it. Most email clients have a junk mail filter, and you may have indicated to your email client what is junk mail and what is not junk mail. You are training the algorithm with what you consider to be junk mail versus not junk mail. After a training period, your email client automatically recognizes what junk mail is and is not.[clxxxix]

Unlike supervised learning, unsupervised learning has no past or prior knowledge about the data you are feeding the algorithm. A classic example of unsupervised learning is giving a machine, or algorithm, numerous images. The unsupervised learning algorithm has no specific descriptions about the images to learn from, so instead the algorithm attempts to group the images according to similar characteristics.

If you gave an algorithm a few thousand images, some containing pictures of cats, and others containing pictures of people, the algorithm might look for distinctive features such as pointed ears, and then group all those pictures into one *pile*, and leave the others in a different *pile*. While the algorithm does not know that one *pile* of pictures are specifically cats, because it hasn't been told so yet, it does know that those images share a common characteristic, so are different than the other *pile* of images.

As visually illustrated earlier, deep learning is just a subset of machine learning. It technically is machine learning and functions in a similar way, but its capabilities are different.

It is an understatement to say that the human brain is quite complex. Within the 3 pounds of our brain are somewhere around 86 billion neurons[cxc] (nerve cells), possibly more. There are other cells such as the glial cells (non-neuronal cells in the central nervous system), but neurons are the ones most involved in learning. Neurons are cells that send and receive electrochemical signals to and from the brain and nervous system. They do this at up to 200 mph.[cxci] Neurons are incredibly tiny - recall that we have about 86 billion of them in our skull. About 30,000 of them can fit on the head of a pin.[cxcii]

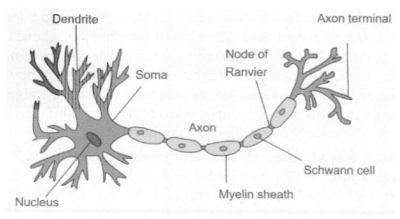

Figure 15 - A BIOLOGICAL NEURON. Source: Wikipedia. Credit Quasar Jarosz[cxciii]

A single neuron may be connected to thousands of other neurons via synapses - the spaces between neurons. It is estimated that a single neuron may be connected to another 5,000 to 10,000 other neurons. Our brain is a sophisticated network of interconnected cells. There are more than 1,000 trillion synapses (a junction between two nerve cells) that mediate neuron signaling in the brain.[cxciv]

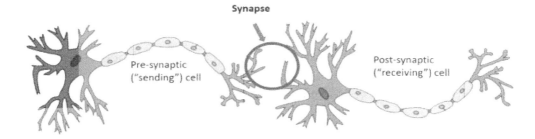

Figure 16 - A BIOLOGICAL SYNAPSE. Source: Wikipedia. Credit Quasar Jarosz [cxcv]

Scientists and engineers are attempting to emulate these biologic processes to create powerful, perhaps ultimately intelligent machines.

Neurons are arranged in columns in the outer layer of the brain known as the neocortex (new cortex). The neocortex is the part of the mammalian brain involved in higher-order brain functions such as sensory perception, cognition, generation of motor commands, spatial reasoning and language.[cxcvi] It's regarded as the more recently evolved part of the cortex. The neocortex is the wrinkly part of the brain with the deep grooves (sulci) and wrinkles (gyri). These folds, technically known as gyrification or convolution, serve to increase the surface area of the neocortex giving us more intelligence. These folds also allow more brain surface area to fit inside of our skull. It's not the bigger brains that have more intelligence, it's the more wrinkly brains.

In an attempt to replicate biological neurons, computer scientists have created artificial neurons. An artificial neuron is basically a mathematical function. A mathematical function takes an input, performs a calculation, and spits out an output. Functions are typically represented in mathematical notation as f(x) = y, where y is the output, f is the name of the function, and x is the input.

Consider a simple function called temperature. It converts temperature from Celsius to Fahrenheit. It might look like this:

temperature (22) = 71.6

You pass the function a value, in this case a Celsius temperature value of 22, and the function outputs a Fahrenheit result of 71.6. You don't necessarily care what's going on inside the function, you just know that you can expect a reliable output each time you pass it an input.

The simplest artificial neuron (also artificial neural network) is called a perceptron. Perceptrons were invented by Frank Rosenblatt in 1958. Frank Rosenblatt was an American psychologist notable in the field of artificial intelligence.[cxcvii] The perceptron is the building block of artificial intelligence.

Artificial neurons are essentially mathematical functions that take inputs, perform a calculation, and only if the calculation meets some criteria, provide an output. This output is the artificial neuron *firing*. In other words, if the input satisfies a condition, they fire.

Consider the following figure, a simplified artificial neuron. It has one input and one output. In addition, it has a weight (1.2) and a threshold (2.5). The input (the incoming signal) is amplified or de-amplified by the weight (1.2). If the weighted input exceeds the threshold, then the neuron will fire.

Weights represent the strength of the connection between neurons. If one weight has a higher value than another weight, it will have more influence on the output.

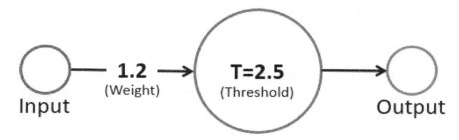

Figure 17 – ARTIFICIAL NEURON

The following table illustrates two scenarios in which our artificial neuron will fire and two scenarios when it will not. Note how the amplified value (the input multiplied by the weight) has to be greater than the threshold value (2.5) in order for the artificial neuron to fire.

Input	Weight	Amplified Value	Will it fire (result > 2.5)?
0.50	1.20	0.60	No
2.50	1.20	3.00	Yes
1.50	1.20	1.80	No
2.80	1.20	3.36	Yes

Figure 18 – ARTIFICAL NEURON TRUTH TABLE

Just like in the brain where neurons are connected to many other neurons, artificial neurons may also be connected to many other neurons. The following figure illustrates such an example where there are now two inputs – Input 1 and Input 2.

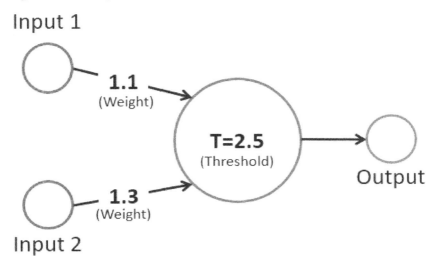

Figure 19 – ARTIFICIAL NEURON WITH MULTIPLE INPUTS

In this example, there are two inputs to this artificial neuron. Each input is amplified by its respective weights (1.1 and 1.3). This neuron will fire ONLY if both inputs exceed the threshold. Input 1 AND Input 2 must exceed the threshold. In computer science we call this an AND condition. Both conditions must be satisfied in order for this particular artificial neuron to fire.

Artificial neurons can have many inputs and the math to determine whether or not to fire can become fairly involved, but essentially for each input, you multiply each input value by each weight, add them all together and this will determine if the artificial neuron fires.

What do we mean by *fire*? It simply means that the condition of the function is satisfied and that we either pass a value from this artificial neuron to another artificial neuron or we output some final value.

When we connect many of these neurons together, we build what is known as an Artificial Neural Network (ANN). In machine learning, Artificial Neural Networks were inspired by the neural network of the human brain.

A slightly more complex artificial neural network is shown below. It contains an input layer, a hidden layer, and an output layer. Every node (the circles) in one layer is connected to every node in the next layer. Each node is an artificial neuron. Just like the brain is an inter-connected network of neurons, an artificial neural network is an inter-connected network of artificial neurons.

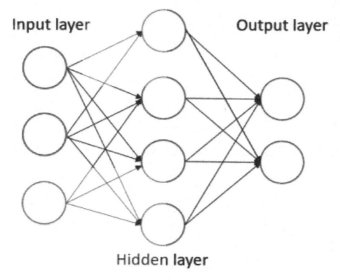

Figure 20 – SIMPLE ARTIFICIAL NEURAL NETWORK WITH ONE HIDDEN LAYER

Deep learning is another type of artificial neural network with many hidden layers between the input layer and output layer. They get their name because they are *deep*; they have many hidden layers.

Deep learning operates more closely to how the brain operates.

Deep learning is still machine learning. It is simply a subset of machine learning that focuses on pattern recognition.

There are different types of deep neural networks (DNN). In a *feed-forward* type of DNN[cxcviii], the data flows in one direction. Data flows from the input layer though the hidden layers to the output layer.

Feed-forward networks are extensively used in pattern recognition and are useful for things like image recognition.

A recurrent neural network (RNN)[cxcix] on the other hand allows data to flow in any direction. This type of network is a *Feedback* network in that data can be fed back into the model. Feedback networks can be very complex and are quite powerful.

The data that is fed back allows the neural network to be dynamic, to update itself until an optimal state is achieved. In other words, train itself. This is known as Back Propagation. You'll recall that earlier we talked about the weights on the artificial neurons. Back propagation is a training method used to update the weights in a recurrent neural network.

Think about when you are reading. Sometimes you have to go back and re-read a word to get the correct context of the sentence. You do this so quickly and automatically that you typically aren't even aware you are doing it. Take for example, the following sentence:

Joe is going to wash his car, tonight.

Up until you read the word tonight, you might have thought Joe was going to wash his car now. By getting that extra bit of context, the word tonight, you now know more precisely when Joe is going to wash his car. You sub-consciously (or consciously) went back and re-read the beginning of the sentence to get the full meaning. This is a simple example of the concept of an RNN.

Recurrent neural networks are very popular for tasks such as natural language processing (NLP) – understanding what humans are saying, handwriting recognition and speech recognition.

We've used a lot of machine learning jargon in this chapter. Let's re-cap and use an example to explain.

Let's say you wanted to create a neural network to recognize handwriting. You start with a collection of images of handwriting characters. This is called your training data. You feed these images into your neural network algorithm. The network hasn't been trained yet so while it may correctly recognize some of the letters, it may miss many of them too. For the letters it does not recognize, you compare the output to the expected output and calculate an error. You then feed that error back into the network, adjusting the weights and repeat as necessary. You repeat the training process until the errors are as minimized as possible.

Said differently, you are tweaking the weights to train the network. After enough training you can then put unknown handwritten characters into the network and the neural network will more accurately recognize them.

We're skipping numerous technical details here for the sake of brevity. In a well-constructed deep neural network, there will be many hidden layers. One layer may be trained just to look at the overall shape of a letter, another the slope of a line in letter, another looking for round shapes, and so on. Each layer passing data to the next layer if the previous condition was satisfied.

This is a sophisticated space, one where a strong background in mathematics and data science is required. Fortunately, a lot of smart people have done a lot of complex work that is now finding its way into everyday devices.

As is often the case with technology, over time, the technology is commoditized and available for the masses.

Artificial Intelligence is all about data, really big data. Data is the very foundation of artificial intelligence. Without training data to train the AI models, the AI systems would simply not be able to learn.

Data is the teacher to the AI student.

Without the rise of big data and the massive amounts of data we are creating thanks to the Internet and the Internet of Things, AI would not be possible, at least not at the scale or pace we are seeing it occur. Data allows AI to learn, to iterate, to fine-tune its predictions and improve its accuracy. Simply put, the more data, the better the AI.

Although we broadly talk about data as the fodder for AI, all data is not used the same. Machine learning is complex, and data serves multiple purposes in training the models.

Generally speaking, data is used in three ways in machine learning.

1. The first is the training data. This is the largest part of your data set. This data is fed into the models and uses it to make predictions.
2. The second set of data is the validation data. This is data that the model has never seen before. This validation data validates whether or not your model is working correctly and may also indicate where the model needs to be fine-tuned further.
3. The third set of data is the test data. This comes last after the training and validation. This is where you ideally do your final tests and the model works as expected.

Finding validation and test data is relatively easy as it's a small data set, but without massive amount of training data, your model cannot be trained, and your AI model will be useless.

This is one of the reasons that companies such as Google and Facebook are making such big strides with AI, because they have access to such huge amounts of training data.

14. THE CURRENT STATE OF AI

"I know that I am intelligent, because I know that I know nothing."
- Socrates, Greek philosopher. 470 – 399 BC

At this point it's worth pausing and taking stock in the current state of artificial intelligence. It's easy to get caught up in all the hype and sensationalism that surrounds it. Let's review the current state of the industry.

In 2019, IDC estimated that "Worldwide Spending on Artificial Intelligence Systems Will Grow to Nearly $35.8 Billion in 2019, an increase of 44.0% over the amount spent in 2018." "Global spending on AI systems will be led by the retail industry where companies will invest $5.9 billion this year on solutions such as automated customer service agents and expert shopping advisors & product recommendations. Banking will be the second largest industry with $5.6 billion going toward AI-enabled solutions including automated threat intelligence & prevention systems and fraud analysis & investigation systems. Discrete manufacturing, healthcare providers, and process manufacturing will complete the top 5 industries for AI systems spending this year. The industries that will experience the fastest growth in AI systems spending over the 2018-2022 forecast are federal/central government (44.3% CAGR), personal and consumer services (43.3% CAGR), and education (42.9% CAGR)." [cc] They go on to say, "The continued advancement of AI-related technologies will drive double-digit year-over-year spend into the next decade."

Artificial intelligence is arguably the fastest growing technology in the world. In 2017 there were 12,000 new patents in the AI field in the United States alone.[cci]

At Stanford University, a group of leading AI thinkers known as the AI100 maintain an index that attempts to provide a comprehensive overview of the state of artificial intelligence. It attempts to measure technological progress in field in much the same way the S&P 500 index tracks the U.S. economy.

The mission of the AI Index[ccii] is to "Ground the conversation about AI in data. A project within the Stanford 100 Year Study on AI (AI 100), The AI Index is an initiative to track, collate, distill and visualize data relating to artificial intelligence. It aspires to be a comprehensive resource of data and analysis for policymakers, researchers, executives, journalists and others to rapidly develop intuitions about the complex field of AI."

The AI Index tracks and measures multiple trends in academia, industry, open-source software and public interest. It also tracks technical assessments of progress toward what the authors call "human-level performance."

Some highlights from the 2017 inaugural report:
- "The number of AI papers produced each year has increased by more than 9x since 1996"
- "Introductory AI class enrollment at Stanford has increased 11x since 1996"
- "The number of active US startups developing AI systems has increased 14x since 2000"
- "The share of jobs requiring AI skills in the US has grown 4.5x since 2013"

Clearly the interest in AI is growing at a healthy rate. Yet, for all the news, all the investments and all the patents, we have a long way to go.

Consider the following request you might make to a small child: "Put your shoes on."

Most children would have very little difficulty understanding that request. They might know where to go to find their shoes, they would recognize their shoes from someone else's, they would know to put socks on before their shoes. In fact, they would even know whether or not the shoes they were putting on required socks. For example, sandals typically do not require socks, whereas other shoes might. And, of course they would know that shoes go on their feet not their head.

Now consider making the exact same request to a humanoid machine. Could a machine find the shoes? Could it differentiate one set of shoes from another? Could it differentiate between a left and right shoe? Would it know to put them on its feet, versus its head? Would it know that it could only put shoes on if it already did not have shoes on, or might it attempt to put shoes over its existing shoes?

There are many tasks that seem simple to us yet are incredibly challenging for machines. Machines are extremely good at doing the same task over and over again, but when you introduce exceptions, such as shoes already on the feet, a machine struggles with what to do.

This is not to say that machines will not learn and adapt much like we do. They will. But this trivial example that we can do so easily illustrates how far away we are from creating truly intelligent machines.

It's important to note that even we humans do not fully understand our own brain, never mind trying to replicate it. For example, self-awareness is still somewhat mysterious. While we may be able to create machines that simulate self-awareness, we have yet to fully understand it ourselves.

If you follow artificial intelligence in the news, you may have seen a story recently that talked about Facebook's artificial intelligence machines (chatbots) and how they had to be shut down after they started talking to each other in their own language.[cciii] It was claimed that two artificially intelligent programs appeared to be chatting to each other in a language that only they understood.

At first blush this might seem quite alarming. It turns out however it was later debunked.

Dhruv Batra, Research Scientist at Facebook AI Research explained in a Facebook post:[cciv] "Agents will drift off understandable language and invent codewords for themselves. Like if I say 'the' five times, you interpret that to mean I want five copies of this item. This isn't so different from the way communities of humans create shorthands." A lack of concern was also echoed by linguist Mark Liberman[ccv]. He stated, "it's unlikely that the language is a precursor to new forms of human speech."

While the idea of AI agents inventing their own language may sound alarming or unexpected to people outside the field, it is a well-established sub-field of AI, with publications dating back decades. Simply put, agents in environments attempting to solve a task will often find unintuitive ways to maximize reward. Analyzing the reward function and changing the parameters of an experiment is NOT the same as "unplugging" or "shutting down AI." If that were the case, every AI researcher has been "shutting down AI" every time they kill a job on a machine."

So, realistically, how far along are we with artificial intelligence?

Michio Kaku is an American theoretical physicist and futurist.[ccvi] He is professor of theoretical physics in the City College of New York and Graduate Center of the City University of New York. In a Reddit (online community) AMA (Ask Me Anything) session, he was asked about his opinion on intelligent machines.[ccvii] His response: "Right now, robots have the intelligence of a bug. They can barely walk across a room. Simple tasks done by humans (picking up garbage, fixing a toilet, building a house, solving a crime) are way beyond what a robot can do. But, as the decades go by, they will become as smart as a mouse, then rat, then a cat, dog, and monkey. By that point, they might become dangerous and even replace humans, near the end of the century. So, I think we should put a chip in their brain to shut them off if they have murderous thoughts."

While machines are very good at certain tasks, they have a long way to go (many decades in fact) until they start to rival humans. It is also unclear if they will ever have true consciousness. That is still very much the realm of science fiction.

There are however many other examples of where machine learning is very capable. For example, one of the areas that machine learning excels is in image recognition. A process described as Deep Visual-Semantic Alignments for Generating Image Descriptions[ccviii], uses a machine learning technique known as Multimodal Recurrent Neural Networks (m-RNNN).[ccix] It is an algorithm that can examine an image and generate natural language descriptions of the image.

Let's say you pass the algorithm an image of a woman playing tennis. The algorithm can tell you that it is a woman, wearing a white dress, holding a tennis racket, while standing on a green lawn. While the system is not perfect, it's hard to argue that it's not impressive.

Similar approaches can take this a step further. Google demonstrated a similar technique where the image components were identified, turned into language and then fed through their language translation engine.[ccx] One could envision a camera for the blind that audibly explained what it was looking at in the user's language of choice.

Photomath[ccxi] is an interesting application that uses the camera of your mobile device. You point the camera at printed mathematical equations, for example in a book, and the app will solve them for you. It can handle complex arithmetic, quadratic equations, linear equations, trigonometry, integration, and more.

Google's AutoDraw[ccxii] is a good example of machine learning to determine intent. As you start drawing it will auto-complete the shapes it thinks you are trying to draw. Let's say you start drawing a four-legged animal, it will auto-suggest a horse, a dog, a giraffe, etc.

Researchers from MIT's Computer Science and Artificial Intelligence Laboratory (CSAIL) created an app called Pic2Recipe[ccxiii] that correctly identified recipes 65% of the time during testing. The team trained artificial intelligence to recognize types of foods. The CSAIL researchers then built a database of over 1 million recipes that were annotated with information about the ingredients. That data was used to train a neural network to find patterns and make connections between pictures of food images and the recipe.

Twitter is using machine learning to crop photos to their most interesting parts.[ccxiv] They call it "cropping using saliency"; saliency meaning whatever is most interesting in the picture. To do this they use the data from academic studies of eye tracking. The eye tracking studies recorded what areas of an image people looked at first. This data can then be used to train machine learning algorithms to predict what people might want to look at.

On a more somber note, an AI that can predict death was given FDA approval in 2017. The algorithm monitors patients' vitals to help predict sudden death from heart attacks or respiratory failure. The algorithm, named the WAVE Clinical Platform, was created by the medical technology company ExcelMedical. According to their website, "WAVE gives early warning of patient deterioration on average more than six hours in advance of when clinicians would otherwise notice."[ccxv] While this may not seem like a significant amount of time, it may be critical to help the patient be more comfortable in their final hours, as well as notify loved ones of the inevitability so that they may be there if desired.

Artificial intelligence is also helping to diagnose Alzheimer's. Alzheimer's is notoriously difficult to diagnose. The only way a doctor can tell for sure if the patient has the disease is to examine his or her brain during an autopsy. An AI system called IDDementia (Artificial Intelligence for Diagnosing Dementia) was developed to help doctors detect Alzheimer's[ccxvi]. Researchers fed the algorithm 191 PET scans of the brains of patients who had been experiencing cognitive impairment. The researchers then went on to teach the algorithm which of these patients had gone on to develop Alzheimer's, and those that had not. There is a protein called amyloid which shows up in patients with cognitive impairment, including Alzheimer's. It is detectable in the PET scans. However, to the naked eye it is difficult for a physician to look at the scan and see which patients may develop Alzheimer's versus a mild cognitive impairment. The AI system analyzed 82 new brain scans and was able to identify with 84% accuracy those who would develop

Alzheimer's in the next two years.

Connecterra[ccxvii], a Dutch company developed a system called IDA, or "The Intelligent Dairy Farmer's Assistant." It utilizes sensors and AI to determine if a cow is chewing its cud, lying down, walking, eating or drinking. These behaviors can predict whether a particular cow has become ill, is less productive, or is ready to breed. Some farmers manage thousands of livestock and determining which animal needs attention manually is very challenging. This type of technology can help improve farming efficiency.

In addition to these few examples, there are numerous other examples of AI doing such things as composing musical pieces for film or games, writing poetry and short stories, beating humans at many types of games, and much more. Just about every industry is starting to see the benefits and challenges of AI.

While many of these approaches are in their infancy relative to what we'll see the coming years, it is clear that there are virtually unlimited applications for artificial intelligence, and that soon artificial intelligence will be indispensable.

One of the ways that machines could learn even faster is by teaching one another. This is the one big advantage that machines have over humans. Obviously, humans teach one another all the time, but it's a relatively slow process. This is not the case for machines. Once a machine gains knowledge it can upload that knowledge to the cloud, where another machine can simply download it.

And of course, machines are not limited by learning from one another, they can also be taught by humans. A great example of this is self-driving cars. There are over a billion drivers on the road. Hypothetically if each of those drivers were in a connected vehicle, their driving behavior could be uploaded to the cloud, where machine learning could parse that data and learn from it. That knowledge could then be downloaded to autonomous vehicles to improve their own driving.

This concept is not new. From December 2010 to January 2014 a project known as RoboEarth[ccxviii] was run to test this concept. Robots could use this cloud-based infrastructure to store and share information with one another. They could collaborate and achieve a common task. The robot might also ask a person for assistance if it was unsure how to perform a task. At the end of the task the robot could share its new knowledge by uploading it to the cloud.

This project demonstrated some of the core concepts in developing a human to machine, machine to machine collaborative model.

I believe this approach will be the de-facto way in the future, in which machines learn from one another. This means that any device with a connection can tap into this *intelligence* in the cloud.

Connections turn *dumb* things into *intelligent* things.

This means that normal, everyday things such as your car, your phone, your cameras, your home, once connected become vastly more capable.

They will learn their skills from other trained devices.

Things will be able to recognize faces, translate between languages, recognize emotion, recognize people, shapes, objects and much more. For example:
- Your security camera in your driveway will read license plates and send them to the cloud for recognition.
- Your front door will recognize faces and know whether or not to automatically unlock.
- Your smart glasses will automatically perform language translation in real-time when needed.
- The same smart glasses will ensure you'll never forget a face or name again by looking up an individual you are talking to and displaying information that only you can see.
- Your connected cup or plate will check the food before you consume it for safety or recalls.

The possibilities are, as they say, endless. These capabilities will become available to any thing with a connection. Everyday things are about to become incredibly *intelligent*.

In addition to access to *intelligence*, the cloud will bring supercomputing abilities to anything with a connection, and everything will have a connection.

Connectivity by itself is not enough, however. Other technological forces are making our connected devices smaller, faster, and cheaper which means that not only will we have vast amounts of intelligence in the cloud, the things themselves will have local intelligence.

In this chapter we learned a little about machine learning. As we've seen, machine learning clearly relies upon technology, and technology in turn is governed by laws. These laws, while predictable, are changing faster than you might expect. As result, technology will change faster than you might expect.

Read on to see how technology is changing at an explosive rate and the implications it will have for intelligent machines.

15. INTELLIGENCE FOR SALE

"The true sign of intelligence is not knowledge but imagination."
- Albert Einstein, Theoretical physicist

Bernard of Chartres was a twelfth-century French Neo-Platonist philosopher, scholar, and administrator[ccxix]. He used to say that "we [the Moderns] are like dwarves perched on the shoulders of giants [the Ancients], and thus we are able to see more and farther than the latter. And this is not at all because of the acuteness of our sight or the stature of our body, but because we are carried aloft and elevated by the magnitude of the giants."[ccxx]

A modernized variant of this is "If I have seen further it is by standing on the shoulders of giants." Simply put, this refers to building on the works of others. This is how society works. Someone, or some organization does the hard work so that others may benefit from it, ultimately moving civilization forward. For example, English scientist William Gilbert established the science underlying the study of electricity and magnetism. Others such as Benjamin Franklin, Nikola Tesla, Thomas Edison and more, did the hard work of discovering and harnessing electricity, so it is a trivial act for us to walk into a room and flick a light switch on. We build upon the discoveries and contributions of others.

The field of artificial intelligence is no different. It is common for scientists and engineers to build on the work of others, and eventually that work becomes commoditized, and is available for general consumption by all.

We are beginning to see this trend now with artificial intelligence and machine learning. There are many smart home devices that employ machine learning algorithms, such as Amazon Alexa, Google assistant, Apple's iPhone or Home Pod, and more. More than one in four U.S. broadband households own a smart speaker with voice assistant.[ccxxi]

However, these are self-contained devices built by huge corporations.

What if you want to build your own applications, devices, or services that performed similar capabilities?

We are starting to see artificial intelligence for sale. And this is just the beginning of an unstoppable trend.

One such example is Algorithmia[ccxxii]. They offer an "AI Marketplace" where you can browse hundreds of algorithms related to machine learning. These algorithms available via API calls, are fractions of a penny per call. APIs, short for Application Programming Interface, is a software intermediary layer that allows applications to talk to each other via a standardized format.

This marketplace contains user-contributed algorithms that can perform tasks such as face detection, face recognition, colorize black and white images, understand intent from natural language, and much more.

Now companies and developers can build sophisticated applications that leverage complex machine learning algorithms through only a few lines of code. Coupled with IoT, this makes for a very powerful combination. For example, imagine you wanted to build a front door camera that could recognize faces. All you need to do is snap a picture of the face, send it to an algorithm in the cloud, get the results back, and determine what to do next; perhaps unlock the door if it is a known face.

This quiet change is the beginning of a significant shift. As we commoditize more and more of these sophisticated machine learning algorithms, and place them in the cloud, devices with a connection will be able to take advantage of these capabilities. This also means that we will see more and more applications and services that offer powerful abilities such as face recognition, intent, object recognition, and many more.

The Raspberry Pi is a credit-card-sized computer that plugs into your TV and a keyboard[ccxxiii]. It is small, very affordable, very capable, and a popular computer with the DIY or maker crowd[ccxxiv].

In 2017 Google announced an initiative called AIY[ccxxv], a combination of DIY (do it yourself) and AI (artificial intelligence). They call it "Do-it-yourself artificial intelligence." These are build it yourself AI hardware kits with accompanying software that allows Raspberry Pi's to perform things such as image recognition and voice recognition. This allows makers to build intelligent devices that can see, speak, and even understand language.

As of this writing, a Raspberry Pi (depending on the model) costs about US$20, the voice kit about US$50, and the vision kit about $US90. For around US$160 a maker can build a device that can see and recognize objects, and understand language using machine learning.

Over the course of many years, millions of dollars were spent in the research and development to create these capabilities, and now they are available to anyone for a fraction of the cost.

We are truly standing on the shoulders of giants.

Over time, artificial intelligence in the products and services we use will come to be expected. I believe that a day will come when you will not use a given product or service because it is simply too *dumb*. That day will come soon.

Over time capabilities such as face recognition, language understanding, and user intent will be commoditized into the computer chips themselves. In 2017 and early 2018 numerous startups received major funding to build AI into chips.[ccxxvi]

Companies such as Intel are building artificial intelligence into devices that can be used in day-to-day tasks. Intel has developed a technology they call RealSense. This hardware device allows devices such as robots to see, understand, interact with, and learn from their environments. The vision processor resides on an Intel developed chip. It uses advanced machine learning algorithms to process the images and generate 3D depth maps. This allows a device to autonomously navigate a space.

In November of 2018, the same chip giant Intel announced the Intel Neural Compute Stick.[ccxxvii] This USB device can plug into a standard computer and costs a mere $US99. The compute stick is packed with artificial intelligence abilities and is designed to help when prototyping projects. The applications for these types of devices range from smart homes, healthcare, robotics, and more. Developers can now focus on their projects while buying the artificial intelligence they need.

The chips in devices such as these are known as neuromorphic chips and enable neuromorphic computing.[ccxxviii] Neuromorphic computing (or engineering) was developed by Carver Mead, an American scientist and engineer, in the 1980's. Neuromorphic computing is an attempt to "mimic neurobiological architectures present in the nervous system."[ccxxix] You may also hear terms such as a "brain-on-a-chip" hardware. But no matter the term, these are all attempts to emulate biology and simulate the human brain through hardware and software.

The key difference between these new types of processors and the ones used in your computer today is that they process data in an analog, rather than a digital fashion. In other words, instead of computing digitally, in a binary fashion, they compute using analog signals. They work with different levels or intensity of signals, just like our brains do.

Although the idea of neuromorphic chips has been around for decades they are only now coming into fruition. These new types of chips herald the birth of practical neuromorphic computing. A neuromorphic chip is one that mimics, albeit in a simplified way, the functioning of neurons and synapses in the brain. Instead of having to write complex code or connect to a service, the chips themselves, in your favorite gadget, will have on-board *intelligence*.

While these chips have limitations, in that they are not yet general-purpose AI chips, and are certainly not even close to the sophistication or power of the human brain, it is a sign of things to come. In the coming years neuromorphic chips will be common in all of our devices. Every day things will have significant capabilities and will be intelligent.

This cannot be overstated. We are building *intelligence* into everything.

16. RISE OF THE MACHINES

"What we should be more concerned about is not necessarily the exponential change in artificial intelligence or robotics, but about the stagnant response in human intelligence."

- Anders Sorman-Nilsson. Futurist

You may have some reservations or concerns about the future of AI. Many people do. There have been no shortage of dystopian books and movies painting a dark future when it comes to machine intelligence, and recently a number of industry leaders and pundits have come forward raising concerns about the future of intelligent machines. Some of the most intelligent people in the world are deeply concerned that one day in the not-so-distant future the robots could rise up against us, posing a threat to the very existence of humanity.

There is growing concern that artificial intelligence will be placed into military devices, such as autonomous drones and robotics. These leaders are so concerned that several them have written an open letter to the United Nations, urging for protection from autonomous weapons.[ccxxx]

"We believe that a military AI arms race would not be beneficial for humanity," they wrote, concluding that it "should be prevented by a ban on offensive autonomous weapons beyond meaningful human control."

The letter cautions that these autonomous weapons "threaten to become the third revolution in warfare", with the first two being gunpowder and nuclear bombs.[ccxxxi]

The letter concludes with: "Once developed, they will permit armed conflict to be fought at a scale greater than ever, and at timescales faster than humans can comprehend. These can be weapons of terror, weapons that despots and terrorists use against innocent populations, and weapons hacked to behave in undesirable ways. We do not have long to act. Once this Pandora's box is opened, it will be hard to close."

While I agree that artificial intelligence in military applications must be considered with great caution, I also believe it to be an inevitability, because ultimately some country will employ artificial intelligence and an AI arms race will begin.

In 2017, Elon Musk expressed concern during a Vanity Fair interview.[ccxxxii] He used a strawberry picking scenario to illustrate his concern. He said, "Let's say you create a self-improving AI to pick strawberries and it gets better and better at picking strawberries and picks more and more and it is self-improving, so all it really wants to do is pick strawberries. So, then it would have all the world be strawberry fields. Strawberry fields forever." In other words, no room for humans.

During an interview at the AeroAstro Centennial Symposium in 2014, Musk said: "I think we should be very careful about artificial intelligence. If I had to guess at what our biggest existential threat is, it's probably that. So, we need to be very careful. I'm increasingly inclined to think that there should be some regulatory oversight, maybe at the national and international level, just to make sure that we don't do something very foolish."

Tim Berners-Lee, best known as the inventor of the World Wide Web, has also expressed his concerns. At a conference in London in 2017, he spoke about the scenario where artificial intelligence could become the new 'masters of the universe' by creating and running their own companies better and faster than humans.[ccxxxiii]

In 2016, the late professor Stephen Hawking, while speaking at the opening of the Leverhulme Centre for the Future of Intelligence at Cambridge University, outlined his concerns of Artificial Intelligence: "I believe there is no deep difference between what can be achieved by a biological brain and what can be achieved by a computer. It therefore follows that computers can, in theory, emulate human intelligence, and exceed it."

Hawking offered a balanced perspective. He spoke of two possible scenarios, one that included disease and poverty eradication, and the other scenario of autonomous weapons and machines uncontrollable by humans.

He stated: "In short, the rise of powerful AI will be either the best, or the worst thing, ever to happen to humanity. We do not yet know which."

This was not his first insight about artificial intelligence. During a BBC interview in 2014 he cautioned that artificial intelligence could end mankind: "The development of full artificial intelligence could spell the end of the human race."[ccxxxiv]

"It would take off on its own and redesign itself at an ever-increasing rate. Humans, who are limited by slow biological evolution, couldn't compete, and would be superseded," he added. (We'll see later in this book how that might not actually be the case.)

In 2015, he spoke at the Zeigeistminds conference and outlined what he believed the timeline for artificial intelligence growth would be. He said: "Computers will overtake humans with AI at some point within the next 100 years. When that happens, we need to make sure the computers have goals aligned with ours."[ccxxxv]

Other industry luminaries have provided alternative views. Eric Schmidt, the chairman and previous CEO of Google, sees a brighter future for artificial intelligence. In 2015 at a SXSW (South by South West) conference he provided a more optimistic view about the future of AI[ccxxxvi]: "I think that this technology will ultimately be one of the greatest forces for good in mankind's history simply because it makes people smarter. I'm certainly not worried in the next 10 to 20 years about that. We're still in the baby steps of understanding things," Schmidt said. "We've made tremendous progress in respect to [AI]."

He highlighted positive uses of artificial intelligence, such as Google Voice and Google's translation services. "Stuff beyond that is, at this point, really speculation," Schmidt said.

In 2015, Microsoft chairman Bill Gates, in an interview with the BBC[ccxxxvii], expressed his own concerns. Gates said "I am in the camp that is concerned about super intelligence. First the machines will do a lot of jobs for us and not be super intelligent. That should be positive if we manage it well. A few decades after that though the intelligence is strong enough to be a concern. I agree with Elon Musk and some others on this and don't understand why some people are not concerned."

There are many other examples, some positive, some negative. But this generally captures the sentiment of some of our more outspoken leaders.

Time will tell whether or not this dystopian future comes to pass, but personally, I believe that many of these concerns are overblown. Let's say machines do become super-intelligent, even more so than humans. Why do we automatically assume they will be malevolent? Do we think that it is because they will follow our own history of behavior? Even humans, while we have a violent history, are ultimately good. History has shown that we try to advance ourselves in a positive way. While we certainly have made many mistakes and have some messes to clean up, most people would agree that life is better today than it was a few hundred years ago. Perhaps an intelligence greater than ours will understand that war is not the answer – no one truly wins.

I'm reminded of the 1983 movie, WarGames.[ccxxxviii] An intelligent computer was designed to wage war with the enemy. By playing thousands of iterations of a game of tic-tac-toe it concluded that there was no winner in this type of scenario. Could intelligent machines not come to that same conclusion?

Many have expressed concerns that machines will make many jobs done by humans obsolete, and they will.[ccxxxix] But I believe that will only serve to elevate humanity. History is full of examples where machines have taken away jobs from humans, but ultimately humanity has benefited from it. Consider that technology has already taken over 90% of the jobs that humans used to do.[ccxl] From farming to railroads, millions of jobs have been lost to machines. There is no shortage of things for humans to work on next. Food production, water distribution, and climate change are just a few pressing examples that will require our attention. New opportunities such as green energy production, space travel, and countless others will require future workers, many of which cannot be done by machines – at least not yet.[ccxli]

I believe that our fears about the dystopian future are clouded by what we have read in books and seen in movies. Arguably, an alternative scenario is just as likely. Intelligent machines could become a new class of citizens, with a desire to improve the world, rather than destroy or take over. Why let dystopian science fiction shape our future?

We have just scratched the surface of artificial intelligence. We have much to learn about the brain and how to replicate it, if in fact that is even the correct approach. It is our only model for intelligence at this point, but we may very well stumble upon better models. We may also find that artificial intelligence arrives at an intelligence model we cannot currently comprehend. After all, AI has an ability that we humans do not yet have, the ability to connect via a vast inter-connected network of intelligence using the Internet. As billions of new devices connect to the Internet, and as these devices gain ever more intelligence, we are building a global inter-connected intelligence that could one day operate as a single unit. Today this is the material for science fiction, but in the coming years science fiction may very well become science fact.

There is no evidence that intelligent machines will take over or do away with humans it is pure speculation at this point. This is not to say that we should be blind to the advances of AI, we need to monitor the advances closely.

Artificial intelligence is not magic. These are simply very sophisticated algorithms processing massive amounts of if/then logic.

I would argue that consciousness is a prerequisite for intelligence, so unless we figure out how to make a machine conscious, general artificial intelligence is a long way off.

Christof Koch, president, and chief scientist of the Allen Institute for Brain Science in Seattle echoes this sentiment. More specifically, he notes that conventional computers will never be conscious. This is because the underlying hardware that we use to make modern computers is insufficient – something else is needed altogether – a completely different type of hardware.

Even if we were able to simulate every tiny biological detail of the human brain, it would not be enough. That simulation would never be conscious he argues. "Consciousness is not about computation; it's a causal power associated with the physics of the system."[ccxlii] Koch goes on to say "The theory predicts that if we create a machine with a very different type of architecture, it might become conscious. All it needs is a high degree of integrated information. Neuromorphic computers or quantum computers can, in principle, exhibit a much higher degree of integrated information. Maybe they will lead us to conscious machines."[ccxliii]

In the chapter, "Intelligence for Sale", we learned a little about neuromorphic computers, devices that "mimic neuro-biological architectures present in the nervous system[ccxliv]", but we have not yet spoken about quantum computers. Quantum computers may very well be the holy grail for creating intelligence that rivals and perhaps surpasses human intelligence. In the next chapter we will explore some of the realities of quantum computing and why it might pave the way for the ultimate artificial intelligence, artificial generalized intelligence (AGI).

In the meantime, there should be no fear of a machine uprising anytime soon.

17. A QUANTUM LEAP

"Artificial intelligence will reach human levels by around 2029. Follow that out further to, say, 2045, we will have multiplied the intelligence, the human biological machine intelligence of our civilization a billion-fold."

- Ray Kurzweil, American inventor, futurist, author

While artificial intelligence is emerging as a powerful tool, it is limited in its versatility. An AI algorithm that excels at classifying cats in pictures might fail miserably at recognizing handwriting. These are tasks that the human brain does quite effortlessly. This is because the human brain has *generalized* intelligence. In other words, you can place a human in many different situations and the same general brain design that we all share adapts to many situations. While each of us may learn different skills, have different training, or end up in different occupations, at the core, we all share the same type of brain architecture. You can think of the brain as a sort of a "one size, fits all" model.

This is the goal for many computer scientists – to build an AI model that is generalized. This is an incredibly powerful notion. A generalized AI model means that a computer, a robot, a machine could go into any situation, learn, and be useful. Much like a human, the machine would observe, learn, and adapt to the situation. No longer would specialized algorithms be needed for specific tasks or situations. This intelligence is known as Artificial General Intelligence (AGI).[ccxlv]

AGI refers to the notion that "a machine that has the capacity to understand or learn any intellectual task that a human being can."[ccxlvi] AGI is sometimes referred to as strong AI, which contrasted to weak AI, does not perform human-level cognitive tasks. Weak AI is the most common form of AI today. As we've seen, AI today is clearly not at the level of a human brain and it may be many decades before it is – if at all.

One of the emerging technologies that may challenge that is quantum computing. Quantum computing takes advantage of some very unusual aspects of quantum physics to enable computing at an entirely different scale. A scale that perhaps is well-suited for the creation of an intelligent machine.

It's worth noting that quantum computing is still very much in its infancy, and while some companies have claimed to have made some significant breakthroughs in the technology[ccxlvii], it may be decades until we have general purpose quantum computers in our businesses and our homes. As with any new technology, there is usually a lot of hype before there is a lot of impact.

Quantum computers are expected to provide computational power that far exceeds classical computers. Classical computers compute using bits, whereas quantum computers compute using qubits (quantum bits). These bits may be an electron or a particle. With enough qubits, perhaps around 100, a single quantum computer could have more computing power than every computer on the earth combined.[ccxlviii]

Quantum computers are incredibly powerful because they exploit the strange phenomenon of quantum physics.

The first such phenomenon is superposition.

Recall that in classical computing a bit represents a state of 0 or 1. A bit has two states, it's Boolean. It's either true or it's false. It's on or it's off. It's like a simple light switch. This is not the case with a qubit in superposition. When a qubit is in a state of superposition it is in a probabilistic state. It might be a 0, it might be a 1, or more strangely a superposition of the two states. It's more analogous to a dimmer switch that a simple on/off light switch.

Until the state of the qubit is measured, the qubit can be in multiple states at the same time.

The second phenomenon in quantum computing is entanglement.

Quantum entanglement occurs when two particles (qubits for example) become linked. Whatever happens to one immediately affects the other, regardless of distance. Although scientists have only been able to entangle particles in labs over a few miles, particles can be separated by vast distances.[ccxlix]

Initially Albert Einstein dismissed quantum entanglement as "spooky action at a distance", but relatively recently it has proven to be a legitimate quantum phenomenon and often repeated in labs. In July 2019, physicists at the University of Glasgow in Scotland, unveiled a photo of quantum entanglement. The photo shows entanglement between two photons that interact briefly.[ccl]

In addition to being a core enabler of quantum computing, quantum entanglement may one day serve as a foundational element of a quantum Internet.[ccli]

Superposition and quantum entanglement are what makes quantum computers scale exponentially faster than a classical computer.

With a classical computer, adding more bits only makes it slightly faster, but adding qubits to a quantum computer is a very different story.

In a quantum computer, adding a single qubit doubles the total power of the quantum computer. The formula is 2^n where n is the number of classical bits. So,

3 qubits = 2^3 or 8 classical bits

4 qubits = 2^4 or 16 classical bits

10 qubits = 2^{10} or 1024 classical bits

and so on.

The following table illustrates this computing growth potential:

Qubits	Equivalent Classical Bits
1	2
2	4
3	8
4	16
5	32
10	1024
20	1,048,576
30	1,073,741,824
40	1,099,511,627,776
50	1,125,899,906,842,620
100	1,267,650,600,228,230,000,000,000,000,000

Figure 21 – COMPARISON OF QUBITS TO CLASSICAL BITS

It's easy to see the exponential curve in this table.

There are many issues to overcome still with quantum computers. They are large, expensive, require significant cooling, and require specialized environments in which to operate. They have limited utility and limited capabilities. Quantum computers are "delicate" and must be shielded from external influences and cooled down to almost absolute zero. Absolute zero is

-273.15 degrees Celsius on the Celsius scale, and at absolute zero atoms stop moving.[cclii]

Any interaction with the computer can disrupt it and cause errors. Simply observing the computer can affect the result. One of the biggest challenges is decoherence. Decoherence is the process in which the environment interacts with the qubits. This interaction can cause the qubits to change their quantum states, causing information stored by the quantum computer to be lost.

Scientists and physicists are slowly figuring out how to work around these limitations and it is only a matter of time until quantum computers become more stable and reliable.

As history has shown, we have been down this road before. It was only a few decades ago that some of those same limitations (size, cost) described the average classical computer. Now we have one in most homes, and in most pockets.

It is unlikely quantum computers will replace traditional silicon computers anytime soon, and they may never replace them. Both types have their uses and they will likely co-exist for a long time to come.

If we can overcome these challenges, and I have little doubt that we will, the applications for quantum computing are immense. We will be able to simulate the entire planet in incredible detail. We will be able to predict weather patterns and save lives by predicting outcomes weeks in advance. We will be able to orchestrate traffic, be it drones, flying "cars" or autonomous vehicles at scale. We will unlock the secrets of the universe by analyzing petabytes of physics data. We will develop new energy solutions, new medicines, and perhaps even truly intelligent machines.

Quantum computers might yield a more inter-connected platform for an intelligent machine more efficiently than a classical computer. They may be the breakthrough that an artificial generalized intelligence needs.

Physicist Roger Penrose, of the University of Oxford, and anesthesiologist Stuart Hameroff, of the University of Arizona, proposed such a notion in 2013.[ccliii] The brain may very well act as a quantum computer. While there is no scientific evidence as yet to support such a notion, the idea is intriguing.

Penrose and Hameroff are not the only ones pondering this question. UC Santa Barbara theoretical physicist Matthew Fisher[ccliv], and scientific director of the Quantum Brain Project (QuBrain) are asking the same question. Thanks to a $1.2 million grant, Fischer seeks to find answers through rigorous experimental tests.[cclv]

This chapter was an intentional oversimplification of quantum computing to introduce the topic. The physics and science involved are significant and countless billions will be invested into the field until quantum computing becomes mainstream, but the main point remains - if we can build cost-effective, scalable, general purpose quantum computers, they will dwarf every computing device that has come before and may very well lead to true artificial generalized intelligence, which in turn may lead to intelligent machines.

18. HUMAN 2.0

"We've been merging with tools since the beginning of human evolution, and arguably, that's one of the things that makes us human beings."

- Franklin Foer, American writer

It's not just the machines that are evolving. We are. Not simply in the biological sense but accelerated by our command of technology. Technology is finding its way into our lives in a much more intimate fashion than ever before. It is changing how we work, how we play, how we live, and may very likely even change how we define what it is to be human.

Using technology to improve our lives is obviously not new. Since we picked up the first rock to use as a crude hammer, we've always found a way to amplify our innate abilities with technology.

Technology is becoming ever smaller and more densely packed with capabilities. History has shown that things impossible today, will be commonplace tomorrow.

We have begun to build a more personal relationship with technology. About a decade ago, in 2007, the Quantified Self movement began.[cclvi] This movement, made possible through the emergence of wearable technology, sought to provide insight into a person's daily life through data acquisition. Automated data acquisition was made possible via the use of wearable trackers that monitored a wearers step. Over time, these wearables have incorporated more sensors to measure metrics such as heartrate, sleeping patterns, galvanic skin response (which help to indicate stress levels), and even glucose levels. Increasingly sophisticated sensors will likely be developed that give us more insight into our bodies. Coupled with predictive algorithms and machine learning techniques, users will be able to predict illnesses, repetitive stress disorders, and more finely tune their exercise and food regimens.

Humanity is on a continuum of self-improvement though technology. While a continuum is not neatly packaged into distinct phases, by definition, there are four major phases I believe we are going through.

The first phase I call the adornment phase. Humans adorned themselves with cosmetics, tattoos and jewelry in an effort to show wealth, social status, or make themselves more attractive to others. In many ways, this has not changed. Some of the earliest known forms of human adornment were small shell beads, like the shell beads found in Skhul, Israel that date 100,000 to 135,000 years ago. There's evidence that Egyptian women had tattoos on their bodies and limbs around 6,000 years ago. Figurines and female figures represented in tomb scenes display tattoos on their bodies. Small bronze implements believed to be tattooing tools were discovered in the town of Gurob, to the west of the Nile, in northern Egypt.[cclvii]

In the modern age, technology has allowed us to enter the second phase of self-improvement, the wearable phase. From smart watches to augmented reality glasses, we "enhance" ourselves with technology to amplify our abilities or gain insight into our bodies that would otherwise be impossible.

There is a lot of experimentation going on with wearables currently. Testing different form factors, different features, different sensors, etc. The challenge with wearables is that they know little about the wearer. They know more about what they are doing vs. what the user is doing, in other words, they tell you what *they* are doing, not how *you* are doing. This is changing. Devices are transitioning from simply being wearables to aware-ables.

No matter the design, I argue that there are three traits that a wearable needs to make it *aware-able*. I call them the three "C"s They are:

1. Contact
2. Connections
3. Context

First, contact. This refers to contact with your body. After all, how can a sensor really know how you are doing without an intimate connection with you. It is becoming standard for a wearable to have a heartrate monitor on it, and over time we'll see many more sensors that provide even greater insight into the biological functions of the body.

The MC10 BioStamp is an intriguing device that consists of a small, yet powerful collection of sensors designed to measure human physiological data.[cclviii] Designed to be worn on the skin and transmit data to your smartphone via Bluetooth, the MC10 BioStamp is a good example of a device that exemplifies contact with the body. The manufacturers of this device claim that while "traditional electronic devices are rigid, bulky and fundamentally mismatched to the properties of the human body, the MC10 bio stamp is thin, flexible, and built to stretch, bend and twist seamlessly with our bodies." I agree with this philosophy; technology should conform to us, not the other way around.

During the Apple event in September of 2018, Apple announced a new wearable, the Apple Watch Series 4. Among numerous other features, they announced and demonstrated a number of heart rate-related features. Included were a clever combination of sensors and software that could detect a low heart rate, a rapid heart rate, atrial fibrillation (which is a quivering or irregular heartbeat that can lead to blood clots, stroke, heart failure and other heart-related complications), and even electrocardiogram (ECG) reading[cclix]. The electrocardiogram is particularly intriguing as it's the first over-the-counter device in the US to offer these capabilities. Millions of people around the world suffer from heart-related issues and these types of sensors may offer an early warning system to those affected.

In September of 2018, Jason Perlow, the Senior Technology Editor for ZDNet, wrote about how the Apple watch saved his life.[cclx] He was involved in an Apple heart rate study, and a few days into it, he received a notification of an irregular heart rhythm. He contacted a doctor and found that there were indications he might have Atrial Fibrillation (AFib). This common form of heart arrhythmia affects tens of millions of people worldwide and learning about it early on may have saved his life. This type of early notification was made possible by the small size of the sensor and the intimate contact it had with his body.

Wearables will evolve to know *how* you are doing, not simply *what* you are doing.

The next trait aware-ables need is "connections." More specifically, connections to the internet. As will see shortly, connections turn *dumb* things into *intelligent* things.

Consider a heartrate sensor embedded in a wearable. Monitoring your heartrate is useful; it lets you know when you are in the zone when exercising and may even warn you when your heartrate is irregular or unusual. But what if you could compare your heartrate to millions of others to see if that irregular heartrate was unusual or perfectly normal for your demographic? A connected wearable provides that ability. By sending your heartrate data to the cloud, you could compare it to others, analyze it, and see if it's normal, or something you should investigate further.

Today the majority of wearables are tethered to a smartphone for connectivity. The smart phone acts as proxy for the wearable, but as technology shrinks and battery life improves, wearables will evolve to be purely stand-alone devices, and their utility will increase proportionally.

The final "C" is context. Simply put, this is about delivering the right information to the right person (or thing) at the right time to the right place in the right format. To do this, the wearable (or thing) needs to know more about you, for example, what you are doing or where you are.

Consider the simple act of driving. Context would let things around you know that you are driving, and messages would be automatically muted for safety, or may come in as voice instead of text so that they could be read to you. Perhaps you're in a meeting. Context would let things around you know that you are busy, and messages would be muted, or sent to voicemail.

While we can certainly do all this today, the difference here is that this would happen automatically, without human involvement as the devices around you would have context of what you are doing. This will be an expectation of future connected devices.

The third phase after wearables is the embeddable phase. I believe this phase will begin in earnest in the mid to late 2020's. Technology will be small enough and powerful enough that injecting or implanting technology into our bodies will become commonplace. It might be as simple as an electronic contact lens that enhances our vision, or a communication device embedded under the skin.

Embedding technology in our bodies, while controversial, does bring with it some additional advantages. You don't lose it, and you may even be able to charge the devices via your own bodies via glucose biofuel cells[cclxi].

Procedures to embed technology are already fairly commonplace but are typically medical in nature. There are numerous examples where we use embedded technology today to enhance our lives. For example:

- Pacemakers are used to treat arrhythmias (problems with the rate or rhythm of the heartbeat). A pacemaker is a small device that's placed in the chest or abdomen to help control abnormal heart rhythms. The device uses electrical pulses to prompt the heart to beat at a normal rate.
- Cochlear implants can help to provide a sense of sound to a person who is profoundly deaf or severely hard-of-hearing. A cochlear implant is a small, electronic device that consists of an external portion that sits behind the ear and a second portion that is surgically placed under the skin. Eventually, low-power signal-processing chips will lead to cochlear implants that require no external hardware.

- Embedded neurostimulators monitors the electrical activity of the brain and detect abnormal activity that could lead to a seizure[cclxii]. When abnormal activity is detected, the Neurostimulator delivers electrical stimulation to the brain through the leads to prevent seizures.

There are countless other examples, but we are quickly becoming accustomed to combining technology and biology to improve our lives. In addition to medical improvements, implantable devices may give us some remarkable abilities.

In 2009, The University of Southampton demonstrated brain-to-brain communication over the Internet.[cclxiii] Brain-Computer Interfaces (BCI) are electrodes placed on or under the scalp that capture brain signals. These signals are amplified and then translated into commands that can be used to control objects in the real world. This technology has far-reaching applications. From Internet-based telepathy, to helping people with debilitating diseases or locked-in syndrome. LIS, also known as pseudocoma, is a condition in which a patient is aware but cannot move or communicate verbally due to complete paralysis of nearly all voluntary muscles in the body except for vertical eye movements and blinking.[cclxiv]

A few years later in 2015, Andrea Stocco[cclxv] and his colleagues at the University of Washington in Seattle connected two people via a brain-to-brain interface. The people then played 20 questions–type game.[cclxvi] In this game there are two participants, the sender and the receiver. The first participant (the sender) wears a cap connected to an electroencephalography (EEG) machine which records their electrical brain activity. They then pick an object from a selection of choices on their screen, for example, a type of food. The second participant (the receiver) has to guess what the first participant (the sender) selected. They (the receiver) do this by selecting from multiple options on their screen and sending that answer back to the sender via a conventional network connection. The sender (the respondent with the EEG) responds mentally via a yes or no response which is captured by the EEG. If the answer is correct, the computer activates a magnetic coil positioned behind the inquirer's (receivers) head which in turn stimulates their visual cortex to see a flash of light. This flash of light lets them know that the answer to their inquiry (one the 20 questions) was yes. They keep doing this until they guess the correct object.

Although this particular game had a limited degree of interactivity, it is thought to be one of the first to demonstrate a linkage of two brains that allowed one person to guess what the other person was thinking. (The endnote referenced above contains a link to a video which illustrates this process more clearly.)

In 2018, the same team announced they had created a brain-to-brain network which allowed a small group to play a collaborative Tetris-like game. Of significance is the ability for multiple people to participate in this "social network of brains."[cclxvii]

In November of 2018, PLOS ONE, a web site dedicated to "original research from the natural sciences, medical research, engineering, as well as the related social sciences and humanities that will contribute to the base of scientific knowledge" published a paper entitled "Cortical control of a tablet computer by people with paralysis."[cclxviii] In this paper, the team reported the "first brain implant system that lets patients use their thoughts to navigate an off-the-shelf Android tablet." One of the subjects, a musician known as T6 was able to send emails, chat with other patients, perform web searches, and even shop online.[cclxix]

What's remarkable is that she did all of this by thought alone.

While these technologies are still in the early stages of development, the implications for these advancements are profound. Disabled or paralyzed people could control wheelchairs, exoskeletons, and robotic devices. Surgeons could control robotic devices over the Internet to perform tele-operations. Humans could communicate with each other by thought alone. While we're perhaps decades from these types of advances becoming commonplace, embeddable technology brings with it some intriguing applications.

A small group of individuals known as biohackers are already experimenting with embeddable technologies. A few examples include:

- DIY biohacker Rich Lee had sound-transmitting magnets implanted into his ears so he can compensate for his loss of vision by learning to echolocate.[cclxx]
- Amal Graafstra had RFID (radio-frequency identification uses electromagnetic fields to automatically identify and track tags attached to objects) implants in his hands which he uses to unlock his car, computer and door to his Seattle home.[cclxxi]
- Tim Cannon has taken wearable technology to the next level, by implanting a large monitoring device into his arm. This sensor can connect wirelessly to an Android device, read biometric information such as temperature, and send him a text message if he's suffering from a fever, for example.[cclxxii]

The utility of some of these examples may be questionable, but DIY biohackers are experimenting with all sorts of *crazy* concepts which may one day be considered quite normal, and generally accepted. Not long ago tattoos were considered quite risqué, yet today about 30% of Americans sport a tattoo.[cclxxiii] I would not be surprised to see embeddables follow a similar path.

Some companies have started implanting chips into their employees. Three Square Market, a technology company that provides self-service mini-markets to hospitals, hotels, and company break rooms implanted chips into 80 employees.[cclxxiv] These employees volunteered to have the chip injected into their hands.

These chips are about the size of a large grain of rice and contain no battery. They are RFID chips that get temporary power and activate when waved near an RFID reader. This is exactly the same technology you might find when using an access card to enter a secure building. The chips contain a unique ID that is transmitted when activated. This ID can then be looked up by a computer system to determine what privileges are associated with that particular chip.

In Sweden, the adoption rate is even higher. Thousands of people have had these same chips inserted which can function as contactless credit cards, rail cards, and more.[cclxxv]

While there are privacy groups that condemn such activities, it is clear that an embedded chip can bring with it some significant value. These chips can allow a user to gain access to a locked door via a wave of their hand. No more lost or forgotten door access cards. The same chip can be used to pay for food, train tickets, unlock computers, and much more. And, when you leave the company, it is a quick procedure to have the chip removed.

The fourth, final, and arguably most controversial phase (at least for now) is the replacement phase. This will likely begin in the late 2030's. The major difference between the embeddable phase and the replacement phase is that in the embeddable phase, we embed technology to fix an issue, or enhance an ability out of *necessity*, whereas in the replaceable phase we choose to upgrade or augment our biological self out of *desire*.

This notion may be hard to comprehend now – after all, while would someone replace a perfectly good eye, organ, or limb with a synthetic one, when the biological one is perfectly fine?

Consider a few scenarios:
- What if, in the future, you could replace your eye with one that gave

you super-human vision? Perhaps zoom capabilities, infrared vision for seeing better at night, or simply eyesight that never deteriorated. As a precursor, researchers at UCSD (University of California San Diego), and EPFL (École Polytechnique fédérale de Lausanne, a research institute and university in Lausanne, Switzerland) created a telescopic contact lens that gives you the power to zoom your vision almost three times[cclxxvi]. In May 2020, researchers at the Hong Kong University of Science and Technology announced that they had developed an artificial eye that "registers changes in lighting faster than human eyes can – within about 30 to 40 milliseconds, rather than 40 to 150 milliseconds. The device can also see dim light about as well as the human eye."[cclxxvii] This technology will only get better.

- What if you were a professional baseball player and you could replace your pitching arm with one that gave you an advantage over others? An arm that never tired, that threw faster and further, and could calculate optimal trajectories when throwing. Prosthetics are obviously not new, and there are examples of athletes who compete using prosthetic limbs, but we'd hardly consider replacing a perfectly good limb today unless we had to. Future prosthetics may challenge that notion.
- What if others did these types of things, and you didn't? Would you be at a disadvantage? What if your job depended on being able to compete with other *augmented* humans?

In many ways technology has already given us super-human abilities, we're just used to them. The computer in your pocket, your cell phone, affords you remarkable abilities. You can use your voice to summon all the world's knowledge. You can control lights and devices in your home effortlessly with a simple tap. You can communicate with anyone else on the planet without leaving your location, and you can locate yourself on the globe to within a few feet. These are all remarkable things that were impossible a few years ago.

Over time, we won't diverge from technology, we'll get closer to it, and eventually merge with it. This is one of the reasons that machines won't take over. We'll gain incredible abilities through technology augmentation.

As our wearables and other devices become increasingly connected to the Internet, we will become more and more dependent on that connectivity and will ultimately embed those abilities in ourselves.

We will become an extension of the Internet. We will become a member of the Internet of Intelligent Things.

Some refer to this merger of Man and machine as Transhumanism.[cclxxviii] "An international philosophical movement that advocates for the transformation of the human condition by developing and making widely available sophisticated technologies to greatly enhance human intellect and physiology."

Time will tell how intimate we ultimately become with technology, but it is clear that technology will fundamentally shape what we become, and challenge what it means to be human.

Does this redefine what it means to be human? I think not. It's in our DNA to explore, to change. It is literally in our DNA.

From the moment our ancestors picked up a stick or a rock to amplify their abilities, we showed what it meant to use technology to advance ourselves. It's who we are. We shouldn't be afraid of this change, this technical evolution. It's what makes us human, it doesn't redefine us, it's who we are.

19. EXPONENTIAL OPPORTUNITIES

"The greatest shortcoming of the human race is our inability to understand the exponential function."

- Albert A. Bartlett, emeritus professor of physics at the University of Colorado at Boulder

We are living in exponential times. In 2001, in "The Law of Accelerating Returns", American author, computer scientist, inventor and futurist Ray Kurzweil wrote "An analysis of the history of technology shows that technological change is exponential, contrary to the common-sense "intuitive linear" view. So, we won't experience 100 years of progress in the 21st century - it will be more like 20,000 years of progress (at today's rate)." – That's 1,000 times greater than the twentieth century.

The noted futurist and inventor Buckminster Fuller created the "Knowledge Doubling Curve." He noticed that until 1900 human knowledge doubled approximately every century. Today the sum total of human knowledge doubles every 2-3 years[cclxxix], largely in part due to the Internet.[cclxxx] Even if this is an overly aggressive observation, and knowledge doubles every decade, in 50 years, 95% of everything we know will have been discovered in those 50 years.

That is staggering.

Things are changing rapidly. Consider this: 150 years ago, the world was a very different place. There was no electricity, no airplanes, no automobiles, no Internet, no satellites, no smart phones, no computers... you get the idea.

By some estimates our ancestors began trying their hand at farming 12,000 years ago. These early farmers lived in what is known as the Fertile Crescent, the region in the Middle East that includes modern-day Iraq, western Iran, Jordan, Syria, Israel, Palestine, and southeastern Turkey.[cclxxxi]

If we consider this milestone as the beginning of modern civilization, then most of our modern conveniences have been developed in the last 1% of modern civilization. We built upon advances that came before, such as metallurgy, toolmaking, societal groups, and more, but the majority of our advancement has come in a very short time.

This is a great example of exponential growth.

Exponential growth is often very difficult to detect because the bulk of the change happens at the very end of the time.

I sometimes use a chess board analogy to illustrate the concept of exponential growth.

Picture an 8 x 8 chess board, with a total of 64 squares on it. Then place a single grain of rice on the first square. Next place two grains of rice on the second square. Next place four grains of rice on the third square and continue the remaining squares. In other words, on each square put twice as many grains of rice as the previous square. This is exponential doubling.

By the time you get to the 64th square (a doubling of 63 times), that one square will contain 9 million trillion grains of rice. That is approximately 159 billion tons, or 368 times the worldwide annual consumption of rice. 9,223,372,036,854,780,000 grains to be exact.

Let's use one more example to illustrate this concept. Let's say you invested $100 and by improbable luck or skill were able to get a 10% annual return.

While we are fantasizing, let's also pretend that we live to be 200 years old. While impossible today, this may not be as far-fetched as it might seem in the future.

To recap, we have $100 that we are investing, and we get a 10% annual return consistently. We are going to put it the bank for 200 years and forget about it (generally not a good idea to do with your money).

After 50 years we would have $10,000 in the bank. Not bad for the initial $100 investment, but also not exactly retirement money, especially considering we're living to 200 now. However, if you let that money sit for another 50 years, for a total of 100 years, you would then have $1 million from your initial $100 investment. That's not too bad.

But here's where it gets interesting. If you let it sit for another 100 years, for a total of 200 years, you would now have $17 billion.

Visualize 228 pallets stacked with hundred-dollar bills. That's what $17 billion dollars looks like.

This is one of the reasons that investing at a very early age is advantageous.

These example scenarios often surprise people, because our brains are not used to thinking exponentially, we are used to thinking linearly. When you plot an exponential curve, note that the curve is *flat* for about 80% of the growth.

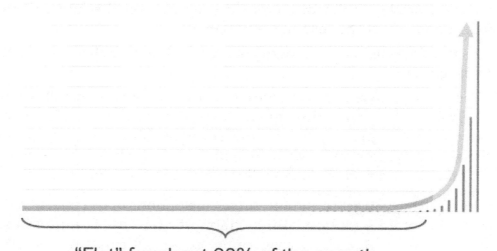

Figure 22 – EXPONENTIAL GROWTH CURVE ILLUSTRATING EMPHASIZING 80%

This is also known as a hockey stick curve, as it looks a little bit like a hockey stick. Notice how quickly things change in the last 20% of the curve.

Figure 23 - EXPONENTIAL GROWTH CURVE ILLUSTRATING EMPHASIZING 20%

This is why predictions that include exponential growth or rapid growth curves are often hard to believe. But exponential growth curves can apply to population growth, technology advances, and return on investments.

So, what does all of this have to do with the Internet of Intelligent Things? Well, the Internet of Intelligent Things consists of a technology underpinning, things like compute, storage, networking speeds, etc. Technology is governed by well understood "laws", and it just so happens that most of these laws are exponential in nature.

20. NOT ABOVE THE LAW

"Technology has advanced more in the last thirty years than in the previous two thousand. The exponential increase in advancement will only continue."
- Niels Bohr, Physicist. 1885 – 1962

Now that you understand exponential growth, let's examine its role in technology. The development and production of modern technological systems factor in compute, storage, connectivity, size, and of course cost. In this chapter we'll investigate each to see the effect they have had as well as their future implications.

Compute

In 1965 Gordon Moore, the co-founder of Fairchild Semiconductor and Intel, observed that the number of transistors per square inch on an integrated circuit (IC) had doubled every year since their invention in 1947. An integrated circuit is essentially a computer chip. More specifically, an IC is a collection of electronic components – things like resistors, capacitors, and transistors, all placed into a single, tiny chip, and connected together to achieve a common goal. They are the little black "chips" you find on just about every circuit board. There are many different form factors, and some are incredibly tiny. There are numerous different types. Some are used as computer memory, others as microprocessors, others as timers, oscillators, and numerous many other functions.

The most popular integrated circuit ever manufactured is the 555 timer. It's called the 555 as there are three 5k Ohm resistors used in the IC, hence the name "555." It's used in a variety of applications that require some sort of timing, for example flashing light emitting diodes (LED).

Figure 24 – SIGNETICS NE555N CHIP. Source: Wikipedia[cclxxxii]

If you were to peel away the black protective plastic case, you would find a number of electronic components, including transistors.[cclxxxiii]

There are different types of transistors, but as we learned earlier, the purpose of a transistor is to amplify or switch electronic signals.

When a transistor works as an amplifier, it takes in a tiny electric current at one end and outputs a larger current. This is really useful for devices like radios where a weak signal may need to be amplified so that it can be heard.

When a transistor works as a switch, it can use a tiny current of electricity to control a much larger current of electricity. Think of a valve used on a large water pipe. A small valve can be used to control the flow of a large volume of water.

This is a key concept in computing and is a simplified explanation of how computer chips work. A chip may contain millions, even billions of transistors all acting as miniscule switches. These switches are either open or closed which means they can represent one of two states a "0" or a "1."

These individual "0" or "1"s are known as bits, short for binary digit. You can string these bits together to create larger values. You've already likely familiar with terms like byte, or megabyte, well a byte is simply 8 bits. Why 8? Historically, the byte was the number of bits used to encode a single character of text in a computer, and for this reason it is the smallest addressable unit of memory in many computer architectures.[cclxxxiv] A megabyte on the other hand is a million bytes, or 8 million bits.

And why the term byte? The term byte was coined by Werner Buchholz[cclxxxv] an American computer scientist. It is a deliberate respelling of bite to avoid confusion with bit.[cclxxxvi]

When you put billions of these binary digits (bits) together you can represent almost anything digitally – music, video, images, HTML pages, video games, virtual reality experiences, etc. In fact, everything in our digital world is based on these simple, but powerful concepts.

Transistors are the fundamental building blocks of modern-day computing.

In the early days of integrated circuit development only a few transistors could be placed on the integrated circuit, but over time as transistors became smaller, more and more could be placed.

The graph below shows the transistor count in microprocessors from 1970 to 2017. Gordon Moore was right; transistor counts have indeed been doubling approximately every two years.

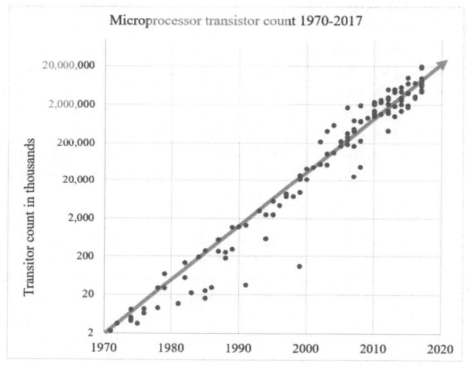

Figure 25 – TRANSISTOR COUNT. Data source: Wikipedia[cclxxxvii]

It's easy to see now how adding more and more of these transistors allows us to do more with digital technology.

As of this writing, tens of billions of transistors in microprocessors are not uncommon. In 2017 IBM announced a new way of manufacturing chips that could hold 30 billion transistors on a finger-nail sized chip.[cclxxxviii]

Some of today's chips have 20 billion transistors, and Moore's law predicts 40 billion by 2020 and 80 billion by 2022. Following this logic, we could see chips that have more transistors than the human brain has neurons within the next decade. Recall that the human brain has about 86 billion neurons. This has significant implications for artificial intelligence and machine learning.

Of course, there is more to artificial intelligence than simply the number of transistors on a chip, but as a technical foundation for powerful computing the numbers are impressive. There will be many barriers to overcome however if Moore's law is to survive. As transistors get smaller and smaller the laws of physics start to interfere. Transistors move electrons around and as the transistors become ever more tiny, and packed more densely together, the electrons experience a phenomenon known as quantum tunneling.[cclxxxix] This causes electrons to *bump* into one another.

As an analogy, imagine an electron as a car, and electronic circuits as the lanes on a road. As you make the roads thinner and thinner, eventually cars are going to run into each other. We cannot change the laws of physics and adjust the size of electrons; all we can do is change the size of the circuits. Eventually physics will catch up to Moore's law. Fortunately, there are other approaches such as 3D stacking of transistors, or new forms of computing such as quantum computing, that will enable us to continue to create faster and faster computers for some time.

Remarkably, in August of 2018, at the Karlsruhe Institute of Technology (KIT – a public research university and one of the largest research and educational institutions in Germany), physicist Professor Thomas Schimmel and his team developed a single-atom transistor.[ccxc] This incredibly tiny electronics component switches electrical current by controlled repositioning of a single atom. The single-atom transistor works at room temperature and consumes very little energy. Conventional quantum electronics components often work at incredibly low temperatures, near absolute zero (-273°C). Being able to work at room temperatures brings significant obvious benefits. Whether we'll ever see this specific work leave the lab remains to be seen, but it does demonstrate how far we can push the laws of physics when it comes to satisfying our computing needs.

In May of 2020, researchers at the National Institute of Standards and Technology (NIST) and their colleagues at the University of Maryland took this a step further and developed a step-by-step recipe to produce single-atom transistors. It turns out that by exploiting a phenomenon known as quantum tunneling, it allows the transistors to become entangled and "opens new possibilities for creating quantum bits (qubits) that could be used in quantum computing."[ccxci]

Storage

Most modern computing devices use some type of storage. Without it, you'd lose all of your data each time the device was turned off. On a computer or laptop this is typically a hard drive. It may be a spinning hard drive or if it's more recent, most likely a solid-state drive (SSD). No matter the specific technology used, we've all grown accustomed to storing our files in folders on our personal computing devices.

Traditional hard drive densities (i.e. how much they can store) is measured in *Areal Density*.[ccxcii] Areal Density is a measure of the quantity of bits that can be stored on a given length of track, area of surface, or in a given volume of a computer storage medium. Simply put, the higher the Areal Density, the more you can store on the disk.

In 1956, IBM introduced the 305 RAMAC (Random Access Method of Accounting and Control).[ccxciii] The IBM 305 was the first commercial computer that used a moving-head hard disk drive. It utilized the IBM 350 disk storage system. The IBM 350 had an Areal Density of 2,000 bits per square inch. The IBM 350 was 60 inches long, 68 inches high and 29 inches deep.[ccxciv] The IBM 350 held 5 Megabytes of data and weighed over one ton. It required a forklift to move.[ccxcv]

Today, a portable hard drive that fits in the palm of your hand can easily hold two terabytes. That's about 400,000 times more space than the first hard drive. Areal Densities have already exceeded 1 trillion bits per square inch.[ccxcvi] That's a 500 million times increase over the first hard drive.

As incredible as this is, physicists, scientists and engineers continue to push the limits. In July of 2018, Physicists at EPFL (École Polytechnique fédérale de Lausanne, a research institute and university in Lausanne, Switzerland) used Scanning Tunneling Microscopy to successfully test the stability of a magnet made up of a single atom. They have shown for the first time that it is possible to store and retrieve information from single-atom magnets.[ccxcvii] Advances such as these could lead to ultra-dense future storage solutions.

Developments such as this are key to sustaining our insatiable desire for data. Data storage needs are increasing at a rate of almost 15 million gigabytes per day![ccxcviii]

One might argue that cloud computing technology diminishes the need to store data locally. While this is true, the cloud providers still have to store the data for you, so this simply moves the storage problem from one place to another.

If you extrapolate these trends out just a few more years, this means that in about a decade, around 2028, you will be able to record every second of your entire lifetime (roughly 80 years) in 4K quality video for a little over $1,000.

Connectivity

I first got online in 1990. I had a 300 bit per second dial-up modem. Today I have a 1 gigabit connection. In 30 years, my home network speed has increased by more than 3 million times and has roughly stayed the same in terms of price.

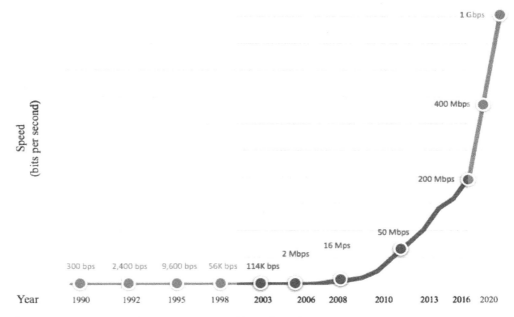

Figure 26 – AUTHOR'S HOME NETWORK SPEED

By now this graph should look quite familiar. It's yet another example of an exponential curve. Notice too, how from 1990 to about 2009, the graph remains relatively flat, and the real speed increases appear in the last 20-30% of the time period.

In 1990 my connection could support one telnet session[ccxcix] (a network protocol that allows a user on one computer to log into another computer). In other words, I could dial up and connect to one remote computer. Today I have well over 100 connected devices in my home, including computers, cameras, televisions, connected door locks, connected lights, and many more. In addition, I routinely stream gigabytes of video and download gigabytes of software.

In 1990, if I wanted use my 300 bps connection to download a 3-4 gigabyte high definition movie to watch later on a flight for example, it would take a little over 30,000 hours, or about 3 and ½ years.[ccc] Today I can download a HD movie in a matter of minutes.

The Internet connection to my home is a fixed, or wired connection, at least today. However, cellular speeds are also experiencing significant growth which may eventually challenge the need for most people to have a wired connection.

As of this writing, we are seeing the emergence of 5G (fifth generation) technologies which promise to provide an order of magnitude improvement in connection speeds. 5G is the term used to describe the next generation of mobile or cellular networks beyond the 4G LTE mobile networks common today.

The table below illustrates the speed differences between the different generations of mobile technologies. Note how 5G speeds begin to rival wired speeds.

Generation	Technology	Maximum Download Speed
2G	GPRS	0.1Mbit/s
	EDGE	0.3Mbit/s
3G	3G (Basic)	0.3Mbit/s
	HSPA	7.2Mbit/s
4G	LTE	100Mbit/s
5G	5G	1000Mbit/s *

Figure 27 – CELLULAR TECHNOLOGY COMPARISION

At Mobile World Congress in 2017, Samsung showcased its 5G Home Routers, which achieved speeds of up to 4 gigabits-per-second.[ccci] These types of speeds could let you download a 100GB 4K movie in under four minutes. It's important to note that these are theoretical speeds in an optimized environment. Real-world speeds will likely be much slower, but even if we come close to gigabit speeds over cellular, they could be game changing. Whether or not 5G will bring gigabit speeds remains to be seen as installations roll out over the coming years. As of this writing, all major cellular providers have plans to launch 5G services with some of them rolling out 5G-capable phones.

5G is projected to be at least 10 times faster than 4G, and possibly much more than that. Today, downloading a high definition movie over LTE (4G) takes about 10 minutes. With 5G, it should take about a second. But 5G will bring multiple additional benefits beyond improved speed, including:

- Shorter delays. 5G should reduce existing cellular latency making things like high-speed augmented reality applications, virtual reality applications and drone control much more responsive.
- Increased connectivity. 5G-equipped cell towers can accommodate more people, and more devices.

To give an idea of how game-changing 5G could be, consider Netflix, a steaming media provider. Netflix recommends a minimum of 1.5Mpbs to steam content[ccciii] (higher quality video requires more). This means that a 1Gbps connection could provide video to 666 displays, or 333 displays at DVD quality or 200 displays at HD quality.

With this type of bandwidth, one could create a completely immersive space where every square inch is covered in HD quality, streaming video. And, if you were OK with lesser quality video, you could cover every square inch of every room in a moderately sized home with a single 1Gbps connection.

While 5G is nearing adoption, early research on 6G has already begun. While 6G is at least a decade away, Huawei, a Chinese multinational technology company, has begun research, and some experts are already guessing what 6G could bring. Some predict that 6G could be 8,000 times faster than 5G. Dr Mahyar Shirvanimoghaddam from the University of Sydney, claims that 6G could "deliver mind boggling speeds of 1TB per second." With 6G "in just one second you could download 142 hours of Netflix movies."[ccciii] While we'll have to wait until the early 2030s to see the real-world impact of 6G, it's exciting to hear what might lay ahead.

The other wireless technology we depend upon for last mile connectivity is Wi-Fi.[cccivi] Last mile connectivity refers to the portion of a network chain that physically reaches the end-user's home or premises.[cccv] As of this writing, the most recent version of Wi-Fi is 802.11ac.[cccvi] 802.11ac can deliver up to 1,300 Mbit/s of throughput. This is in optimal conditions and real-world speeds are typically less. Of note however, is that Wi-Fi speeds have continued to increase dramatically since its creation and release for consumers in 1997.

If you've ever bought a Wi-Fi device such as a Wi-Fi router, you've likely had to decipher terms such as 802.11ac/a/b/g/n. This alphabet soup of technical jargon makes it difficult to understand the differences between the different Wi-Fi versions. As a result, the Wi-Fi Alliance, the organization that manages the implementation of Wi-Fi, has decided to change the terminology into something much easier to follow.

The new terminology is much simpler:

    802.11b (1999) will be known as Wi-Fi 1

    802.11a (1999) will be known as Wi-Fi 2

    802.11g (2003) will be known as Wi-Fi 3

    802.11n (2009) will be known as Wi-Fi 4

    802.11ac (2014) will be known as Wi-Fi 5

And so on.

Version	New Wi-Fi Name	Theoretical speed*
802.11b	Wi-Fi 1	11 Mbps
802.11a	Wi-Fi 2	54 Mbps
802.11g	Wi-Fi 3	54 Mbps
802.11n	Wi-Fi 4	600 Mbps
802.11ac	Wi-Fi 5	1,300 Mbps
802.11ax	Wi-Fi 6	Multi-Gig

Figure 28 – WI-FI NAMING CONVENTIONS

*Real-world speeds are typically much slower due to distance, obstructions, etc.

As this terminology is adopted by hardware manufactures, it will be much easier to see if your Wi-Fi devices are compatible – you'll just have to check that they have the same number. It will also be much easier to tell if you have the latest version as Wi-Fi 6, for example, will be newer than Wi-Fi 5.

Thanks to faster broadband and wireless speeds, downloading content takes a fraction of what it did a few years ago. We can expect speeds to grow at this pace for some time to come.

Martin "Marty" Cooper is an American engineer, and a pioneer in the wireless communications industry.[cccvii] He holds multiple patents in the field. While he was at Motorola in the 1970s, he invented the first handheld cellular mobile phone and led the team that brought it to market in 1983. He is considered the "father of the cell phone" and is credited as the first person in history to make a handheld cellular phone call in public.

Much like Gordon Moore observed the doubling of transistors on chips, Cooper observed that the ability to transmit different radio communications simultaneously and in the same place has grown at the same pace since Guglielmo Marconi's first transmissions in 1895. This led him to formulate the Law of Spectral Efficiency, otherwise known as Cooper's Law. Cooper's law states that "the maximum number of voice conversations or equivalent data transactions that can be conducted in all of the useful radio spectrum over a given area doubles every 30 months."[cccviii]

At least for now, Cooper's law demonstrates that just over every 2 years, wireless network speeds will double. There are also techniques to get more throughput out of wireless devices such as using multiple antennas. This is known as MIMO, or multiple-input and multiple-output.[cccix] MIMO is a method for increasing the capacity of a radio link using multiple transmit and receive antennas with a technique known as multipath propagation. This simply means that the radio signals reach the receiving antenna by two or more paths. In short, a clever technique to get faster wireless speeds.

Researchers are already working on blazingly fast speeds. As early as 2015, researchers at the University of Surrey in England achieved speeds of 1 Terabit per second (Tbps) over 100 meters in a lab environment.[cccx] These are some of the fastest wireless speeds ever achieved. It will be a few more years until this type of technology is out of the lab and in real-world devices, but it's coming. In the coming years you may think nothing of downloading a movie in a fraction of a second.

Size

In his 1999 book *The Age of Spiritual Machines*, Ray Kurzweil introduced his Law of Accelerating Returns, which states that the rate of change in a wide variety of evolutionary systems (including the growth of technologies) tends to increase exponentially. He observed, much like Albert A. Bartlett that exponential growth is counter-intuitive for people as our brains evolved from humans that developed in a linear world. Only recently have we observed technology growing at exponential rates and therefore it is often difficult for us to grasp.

Kurzweil observed that technology shrinks 100-fold in 3D volume every decade. Said another way, if you had a box of a fixed size, every ten years you'd be able to stuff one hundred times as much technology stuff in it as you could before. The box size stays the same, but the technology stuff continues to shrink. And by technology stuff, we mean computer chips, transistors, etc.

Consider how much technology is packed into a modern smartphone: a processor, memory, storage, GPS, Wi-Fi, Bluetooth, accelerometer, biometric sensors, cameras, and more. Just a few decades ago, the technology that fits into your pocket would not have fit into your house. In just a few more decades all of these technologies will fit inside a red blood cell.[cccxi]

This trend means that technology will be small enough and cheap enough that we will be able to take the capability and power of today's smartphone and place it into everyday things, taking up no more space than a grain of rice.

Let's illustrate what that means with a visual example. Say the object below represents some sort of technology, your smart phone if you wish. The object is 25 units x 25 units by x16 units, for a total size of 10,000 units in size.

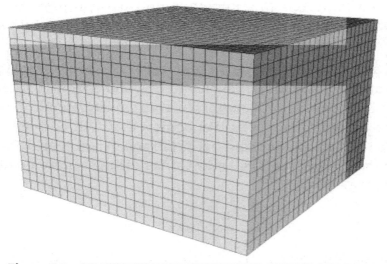

Figure 29 – 3D VOLUME REPRESENTING ARBITRARY TECHNOLOGY

After 10 years, we now have an object that is 100 times smaller than the original. It is now an object that is 5 units x 5 units x 5 units, or 100 units in total, but still has the same capabilities as the original.

THE INTERNET OF INTELLIGENT THINGS

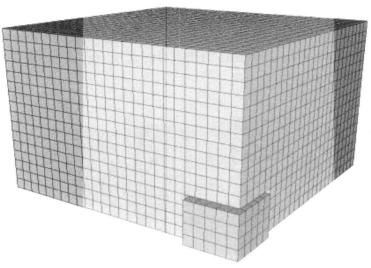

Figure 30 – 3D VOLUME REPRESENTING ARBITRARY TECHNOLOGY AFTER 10 YEARS

After 20 years, we now have a 1 unit x 1 unit x 1 unit object that is 10,000 times smaller than the original but retains the same capabilities as the original.

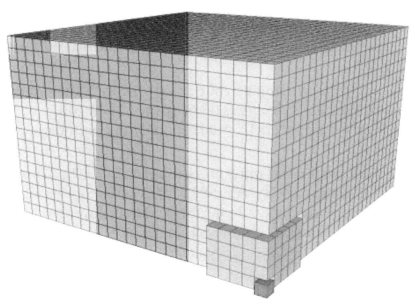

Figure 31 – 3D VOLUME REPRESENTING ARBITRARY TECHNOLOGY AFTER 20 YEARS

And finally, after 30 years, we now have an object with the same capabilities that is 1,000,000 times smaller than the original. This is the small dot at the bottom of the shape below.

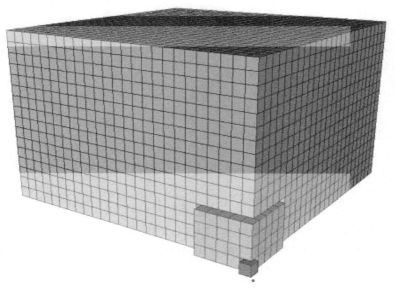

Figure 32 – 3D VOLUME REPRESENTING ARBITRARY TECHNOLOGY AFTER 30 YEARS

This is remarkable. In only three iterations we have something that is a million times smaller, is likely much cheaper, and is more useful due to its size.

History is full of technologies that have followed this trend, from vacuum tubes to transistors, console televisions to ultra-thin wall hanging televisions, mainframe computers to smartphones, and countless other examples.

One of the earliest general-purpose computers was the ENIAC (Electronic Numerical Integrator and Computer).[cccxii] It was released in 1946. In its day it was quite impressive. It could perform calculations in seconds that took humans days to complete. The press called it a "Giant Brain."

It was far from small. The ENIAC contained roughly 20,000 vacuum tubes, 7200 crystal diodes, 1500 relays, 70,000 resistors, 10,000 capacitors and approximately 5,000,000 hand-soldered joints. It weighed more than 30 tons, was roughly 2.4 m × 0.9 m × 30 m (8 × 3 × 100 feet) in size and occupied 167 m^2 (1,800 ft^2) of floor space.

In 1946, the machine cost $400,000[cccxiii] which is about $5.5 million adjusted for inflation in 2018.[cccxiv] It was capable of performing 5,000 cycles per second for operations. In one of these cycles, the ENIAC could write a number to a register (a data holding location in a computer), read a number from a register, or add or subtract two numbers.

Today we have an incredible array of computing options that are significantly more affordable and accessible. Case in point is the ATtiny104. This tiny microcontroller is produced by a company called Microchip headquartered in Chandler, Arizona[cccxv]. (Microchip acquired Atmel, the original manufacture of the Atiny104 in 2016).[cccxvi]

Attiny104 is a microcontroller. A microcontroller differs from a microprocessor in that the microcontroller also contains memory (RAM / ROM) and pins (I/O pins) to connect additional components such as LEDs. Microcontrollers typically have more power-saving features and are often used for less complex applications. There are many other differences, but at its heart, a microcontroller contains a microprocessor.

As of this writing you can buy an Attiny104 for about 0.52 cents (US) in volumes of 100 or more.[cccxvii]

According to the Microchip website, the ATtiny104 "achieves throughputs approaching 1 MIPS per MHz" (This refers to how fast this tiny computer runs). Instructions per second (IPS) is a measure of a computer's processor speed. The "M" in MIPS means million, so 1 MIPS refers to one million instructions per second. Hertz is a measure of frequency or cycles per second. A single hertz is one cycle per second, and the "M" in MHZ also means million, so megahertz refers to one million cycles per second.

So, putting all this together, this little micro-controller, roughly the size of your fingernail (8.65 x 3.90 x 1.60mm) is capable of executing approximately one million operations every second.[cccxviii]

What does all this mean? If you could have bought the processing power of this diminutive Attiny104 in 1964 it would have cost $1.1 billion![cccxix]

1.2 billion Attiny104s can occupy the same space as an ENIAC, and not to mention, the Attiny104 is 200 times faster than the ENIAC!

	ENIAC	ATtiny 104
Year	1956	2018
Cost	$5,500,000	$0.52
Speed (IPS)	5,000	1,000,000
Size (cubic meters)	64.8	0.000000053976

Figure 33 – TABLE COMPARING THE ENIAC COMPUTER TO THE ATTINY 104 CHIP

There are countless other examples I could have used. Indeed, microprocessors and microcontrollers are all around us. From the throwaway musical greeting card to the wearable on your wrist, from the phone in your pocket and even in the adapter used to charge your phone. Our world would be very different without them.

21. INTELLIGENT THINGS ENABLE INTELLIGENT SOLUTIONS.

"I believe life is an intelligent thing: that things aren't random."
- Steve Jobs, founder of Apple

We've seen how the Internet of Intelligent Things could change an individual's day, but what could we use the Internet of Intelligent Things for on a grander scale? How might it change how the world lives? Let's explore how its impact might be more far reaching.

As I write this chapter, sitting in my home in California, a global pandemic has spread around the world killing hundreds of thousands. This pandemic is caused by a new strain of coronavirus known as Covid-19. 'CO' standing for corona, 'VI' for virus, and 'D' for disease. Coronaviruses get their name as the virus is surrounded by a "corona," or crown when viewed under an electron microscope.

Like the exponential laws that govern technology growth, unfortunately viral pandemic growth shares this same curve. By now just about everyone has heard about the desire to "flatten the curve." This is another way of saying slow the exponential growth. While exponential growth may be good for investing money, or new technology, it's the last thing you want to hear about a virus.

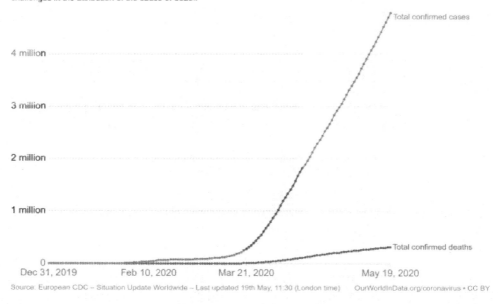

Figure 34 – EXPOENTIAL GRAPH SHOWING GLOBAL COVID-19 DEATHS AND CASES. Source and credit Our World in Data. Licensed under 'Creative Commons' license[cccxx]

While the world is scrambling to overcome Covid-19, a much larger challenge will face us in the coming years.

Around the same time last year, the skies around me where filled with particulate matter from the more than a dozen wildfires that scatter the state, the largest fires in California history. This was the result of an unusually dry winter and arguably linked to climate change. In 2018 many all-time heat records were broken all over the world, resulting in countless fires, and many deaths.[cccxxi] Unprecedented floods hit Japan killing numerous people, a category 5 hurricane blasted Hawaii, and scorching heat waves hit Europe. The list goes on and on, and global temperature projections are alarming.[cccxxii] In 2018, a collaborative research team from China published a new analysis that shows the Earth's climate would increase by 4° Celsius before the end of 21st century. This relatively small degree change would have massive implications. According to Dabang Jiang, a senior researcher at the Institute of Atmospheric Physics of the Chinese Academy of Sciences, "The temperature increase would cause severe threats to ecosystems, human systems, and associated societies and economies."[cccxxiii]

It's likely that we are not moving quickly enough as a species to combat the effects of climate change. In a September 2018 speech at the U.N.'s

New York headquarters, United Nations Secretary-General António Guterres demanded urgent action from world leaders to combat "the defining issue of our time." He went on to say "We know what is happening to our planet. We know what we need to do. And we even know how to do it. But sadly, the ambition of our action is nowhere near where it needs to be." Perhaps most alarming, he stated, "If we do not change course by 2020, we could miss our chance to avoid the disastrous consequences of runaway climate change."[cccxxiv]

The sobering news stories that fill the nightly news and the articles on online media sites remind us how much of an impact humans have on this planet.

While we often talk about how we are affecting our planet, the reality is that we are affecting ourselves. Our planet will go on without us. It was around billions of years before us and will be around billions of years after us. This is not an issue of saving the planet, it's an issue of saving humanity, along with numerous other lifeforms affected by the rapidly changing climate.

We are clearly seeing the impact already. Climate change affects food production. Already one in nine people in the world is affected by hunger[cccxxv], and decreasing food and water supplies will only lead to further conflict, exacerbating the problem.

Consider that it took 99% of human history to reach one billion people, yet less than 1% of human history to reach seven billion people. As of this writing there just over 7.7 billion people on Earth, with projections nearing 10 billion people by 2050 – that's roughly 50% more people than are alive right now.

We are also living much longer. In the 1800's average life expectancy was around 40 years of age,[cccxxvi] while today a person can expect to live on average to about 80 years of age. Of course, numerous factors play into this; disease, healthcare, prosperity, diet, genetics, etc., but generally speaking we have doubled our life expectancy in the last two hundred years.

Not only are there more of us, individually we are placing more demands on our environment. More of us are moving to cities. Today about 50% of the population lives in a city, and by 2050, it is expected that about 70% of the world's population will be urban.[cccxxvii] This will place unprecedented stress on our cities.

Annually, one third of all the food produced in the world for human consumption is lost or wasted, about 1.3 billion tons.[cccxxviii] Yet, we will have 2.5 billion extra mouths to feed by 2050. It is estimated that farmers must produce 70% more food by 2050 to feed the growing population[cccxxix], and climate change will continue to challenge where and when we'll be able to grow food.[cccxxx] Our water supplies are challenged too, with trillions of gallons of fresh water lost to leaks or poor infrastructure.[cccxxxi]

It's pretty clear that we are going to face some social challenges on a scale we've never seen.

However, while much of this seems dire, the Internet of Intelligent Things provides many of the tools needed to address some of our challenges. The old adage you can't manage what you can't measure could not be more applicable.

The ways that humans connect are going to change radically. Connected wearable devices will have huge implications for aging in place, scaling health care systems, and providing unprecedented visibility into the inner workings of our bodies though sophisticated analysis of sensor data in the cloud. From the pills that we swallow to the clothes we wear, from the glasses that help us see to the devices on our wrist, tools like these will monitor our health and provide actionable insight.

The cities we populate will become more aware, more efficient and more adaptive. Buildings will talk to one another and to streetlights and energy systems to manage energy more intelligently. Connected cars will talk to one another warning about traffic jams or accidents and enabling autonomous driving. Emergency vehicles will communicate to other vehicles to optimize their routes to get to victims or to the hospital.

Agriculture will change. Connected machines will plant and harvest our food in the field and in vertical farms co-located in cities, reducing time to consumption and spoilage. Connected, intelligent sensors will tell irrigation systems when water is needed or when a plant needs protection from pests. Intelligent food sensors will alert you before food goes bad, helping to keep it safe and reduce waste.

One company in this field, C_2Sense, is developing sensors that can monitor fruit ripeness and meat/fish/poultry freshness at all stages of the supply chain. C_2Sense sensors are chemiresistors, or chemical resistors. These sensors contain a sensing material which changes resistance based on the concentration of an analyte – a substance whose chemical constituents are identified and measured.

In addition to keeping food safe, new business models could arise. Imagine, for example, walking into a supermarket and receiving a notice on your smart phone incenting you to buy a particular product that is nearing expiration. Your phone knows what you need because it talks to your connected home, and you get that item at a discount if you buy it today.

Intelligent sensors on our pipes and infrastructure will warn us about leaks and check for contaminants, reducing waste and pollution. The American Society of Civil Engineers' 2017 "Infrastructure Report Card" estimates that there are 240,000 water-main breaks in the United States each year, equivalent to wasting more than 2 trillion gallons of treated drinking water annually.[cccxxxii] Recently, a 28-year-old MIT graduate created a leak-detecting robot that could eliminate some of the trillions of gallons of wasted water.[cccxxxiii] This type of technology could be standard on our plumbing using IoT sensors and 5G connectivity to relay the information back. As fresh water becomes scarcer, these types of innovations would easily pay for themselves.

Artificial intelligence will change the face of healthcare and medicine. Secure, tiny devices inside of us will give us insight into how our bodies are behaving. They will talk to intelligent systems that analyze massive amounts of data streaming from our bodies to help us live longer, healthier lives. Of course, this needs to be explored with great care, so our most intimate data is not used against us or exploited for nefarious purposes.

Artificial intelligence will allow us to simulate medicines on virtual copies of ourselves before we ingest them. And AI will help us create new medicines. In February 2020, MIT researchers identified a powerful new antibiotic compound using machine learning. "In laboratory tests, the drug killed many of the world's most problematic disease-causing bacteria, including some strains that are resistant to all known antibiotics. It also cleared infections in two different mouse models."[cccxxxiv] AI will become a powerful tool for healthcare professionals.

One of our largest challenges will be how we manage our environment due to climate change. The first step in managing anything is measuring it. And, the answer may very well be in our pockets. There are billions of connected smartphones packed with sensors that could detect changes in the air and "phone" this information home to create a global climate map. Of course, our planet is blanketed with satellites that give us a birds-eye view but coupled with billions of devices with sensors that are on the ground, it would give us an unprecedented view of our world.

In May of 2018, the Department of Atmospheric Sciences at the University of Washington in Seattle, tested this notion using smartphones to measure air pressure.[cccxxxv] They found that the addition of pressure-sensing smartphones "produced forecast improvements extending several hours."

This same concept could be used to measure air pollution, weather, noise, pandemic spread, and more. Machine learning models could be used to predict trends and provide alerts for storms, poor air quality, and more.

Users could opt-in, perhaps for a discount on their phone bills, or simply to be altruistic. As sensor prices continue to decrease and the technology becomes ever tinier, a typical smartphone may contain dozens of sensors that include environmental sensors. The sensors are not limited to smartphones, they could also be placed in smart watches, clothing, shoes, and more. Smartphones could even measure a user's temperature or pick up coughing sounds. While a single event is less interesting, machine learning models could analyze numerous events to track the spread of the flu or other infectious diseases.

And what about Covid-19? Connected devices and artificial intelligence are already playing a role in helping us tackle the virus.

The genetic material of a virus is stored within a viral protein structure called the capsid. A capsid is the protein shell of a virus. These proteins determine the shape of the virus and understanding the shape is essential to developing drugs to combat the virus. The problem is that examining all the possible shapes of a protein could literally take thousands of years. This is where connected devices and AI come in.

Stanford University's Folding@home distributed computing project uses the idle time of volunteers' connected computers to help researchers develop treatment therapies.[cccxxxvi] Volunteers download software to their computer and while their computer is idle, it works on simulating the process protein folding. This data is then sent back to the Folding@home consortium who can use the result to help with their research.

AI is being used to read computed tomography (CT) scans that can help radiologists reach a coronavirus diagnosis in seconds, rather than minutes.[cccxxxvii]

Machine learning models are being used to predict mortality risks in coronavirus patients.[cccxxxviii] This helps doctors with early identification that may lead to reduced mortality rates.

And, AI is even being used to track how the coronavirus spreads.[cccxxxix]

The use of connected technologies and artificial intelligence is playing a huge role in how we tackle the coronavirus outbreak and these same technologies will continue to be indispensable tools as we face our future challenges.

As the technology continues to become smaller, faster, cheaper, it will become more ubiquitous and more accessible.

While there are countless other issues facing our species as we continue to populate our planet, we've never had more opportunity to use these technologies to help address our challenges. How we grow our food, clean our water, manage our resources, cure diseases, and live our lives is now very dependent upon technology.

Fortunately, that technology is rapidly becoming connected and intelligent, ushering in a new era of opportunity.

22. FINAL THOUGHTS

"The future is not set, there is no fate but what we make for ourselves."
- John Connor, protagonist in the movie Terminator 2

From the humble beginnings of the ARPANET to the vast global connected world in which we now live, the Internet has transformed all aspects of our lives. But that was just the beginning.

The ARPANET gave way to the Internet. The Internet enabled the Internet of Things. And soon the Internet of Things will give rise to the Internet of Intelligent things. Billions of connected devices are creating massive amounts of data. This data is tremendous fodder for machine learning. Connected devices are tapping into these algorithms via connections, becoming *smarter*. Advances in technology means that *intelligence* is becoming cheaper and embedded into everything.

IoT devices create their own *intelligence* – they make themselves smarter. As these connected things proliferate to the point of ubiquity and become smaller, faster, and cheaper, they are creating massive amounts of data, enabling machine learning at unprecedented scale and speed. Fed into machine learning models in the cloud, things can tap into this new *intelligence* in the cloud and then themselves become *smarter*.

This intersection of IoT and AI that I call the Internet of Intelligent Things will give us new tools, new insights, and new capabilities to tackle the growing challenges that lay ahead.

It's going to be an interesting ride.

Just as the Internet served as the foundation for the World Wide Web, which in turn led to commerce, social media, and more, what will the Internet of Intelligent Things be the foundation for? What new opportunities will be created, and how will the next generation of the Internet of Things change our lives once more?

The Internet of Intelligent Things is coming. How will it change your world?

AUTHOR'S NOTE

Although every attempt has been made to be as factual as possible in this book, the reality is that technology changes fast and some information may have become outdated by the time you read this.

Whenever possible, attributions and/or references have been included. This book may contain unintentional mistakes. While great care has been made to ensure the information, calculations, and historical information are as accurate and timely as possible, as well as all sources cited, this book is not a substitute for the source or authoritative historical material.

This book also contains forward-looking projections. Predicting the future is currently impossible. As a result, some of my prognostications may not turn out completely as envisioned, but the topics discussed are notionally and directionally valid. I have included an appendix in this book on the general methodology I use to predict the future.

If predicting the future is of interest to you, there are numerous books on the topic as well as a number of organizations that specialize in this space. The Institute for the Future (IFTF)[cccxl], a Palo Alto, California think tank is one such organization, and one I have had the pleasure of working with on occasion.

I hope this book has helped demystify some of the building blocks of technology, and I hope you enjoyed reading it as much as I enjoyed writing it for you.

APPENDIX – PREDICTING THE FUTURE

It's tough to make predictions, especially about the future.
- Yogi Berra, 13-time World Series champion and member of the Baseball Hall of Fame

As mentioned in the introduction, this book contains forward looking projections. Predicting the future is impossible, however future *possible* scenarios can be envisioned using certain techniques. There are many techniques used to attempt to predict the future as well as many organizations that specialize in it. More organizations now employ futurists as it helps them better understand the trends shaping their industries, which in turn can give them competitive advantage. As the great Wayne Gretsky is attributed to saying, "I skate to where the puck is going to be, not where it has been." This is good advice for those wishing to be one step ahead.

The quote, "It's tough to make predictions, especially about the future", said by Yogi Berra, the famous baseball player turned contemporary philosopher, and attributed to Niels Bohr, a Danish physicist, is spot on because it highlights the dangers of being a futurist.

- In 1895 Lord Kelvin said that heavier-than-air flying machines were impossible. Just eight years later, the Wright Brothers proved him wrong.
- Thomas Watson, president of IBM in 1943 said, "I think there is a world market for maybe five computers." Today, about 1.75 billion people carry a computer in the form of a smartphone in their purses or pockets.
- More recently in 1995, Robert Metcalfe, founder of 3Com and inventor of Ethernet technology said, "I predict the Internet will soon go spectacularly supernova and in 1996 catastrophically collapse."

While being a futurist is not easy, it can be done. In fact, I've made a living out of making predictions for more than 25 years, especially about the future of technology and its impact on people.

My knack for thinking about the future started at an early age. As a young boy in Scotland, I noticed the decaying buildings around me and thought, "Why can't cement heal itself when it cracks?" Just recently, this nascent thought/prediction came true. Henk Jonkers of Deft University of Technology in the Netherlands announced bioconcrete—a new type of self-healing cement that fixes its own cracks using bacteria.[cccxli]

I often get asked how I predict the future. It's definitely not with a crystal ball. Being a futurist is about understanding where the world is now and where it will be tomorrow. And while it's impossible to exactly predict how technology will impact our lives 10, 20, and even 30 years from now, there are several proven techniques that narrow down the countless possibilities to prognosticate a probable future.

Cast a wide net to create scenarios

To understand where we are today, I voraciously consume information. I review more than 120 websites daily for statistics, trends, developments, inventions, and breakthroughs. I also attend industry events, listen to webinars, meet with customers, and read countless books.

From this wealth of information, patterns emerge that allow me to envision future scenarios based on current trends. For example, if I see that the percentage of people buying electric cars is increasing over time, I know that changes to the power grid will be needed to accommodate how people charge their vehicles. I can then begin to think about what the future state will look like and what technologies will be needed to get there.

Backcasting

Once, I have conceived of several scenarios, I then apply a technique called backcasting. This approach is almost the opposite of forecasting. With backcasting, you imagine a future state and then determine the steps or events necessary to get there from where we are today. You start with the end in mind, then move backwards from the vision to the present, and finally move step by step towards the vision and ask yourself, "what do we need to do today to reach that vision successfully." As a simple example, let's take flying cars – a question that often arises for futurists. I've often been asked, "so, when will be have flying cars?"

Here's how you might use backcasting to think through the question. Consider a future world in which flying cars are everywhere. Now, come back today and think about all the things that would be required, for example: Vehicle costs, air traffic control considerations, cost-effective energy sources, acceptable flying ranges, takeoff and landing requirements, safety, collision avoidance technology, networking and computing requirements, alternative solutions, etc., etc. (As you can imagine, it's a long list). Now, for each one of these evaluate and determine the viability and timeframe of each. Together this analysis starts to paint a picture of whether or not this future scenario is possible, and if so, when.

A few successful business leaders are also good at this. Knowing that mobile and video were the future of social communication, Mark Zuckerberg, CEO and founder of Facebook bought Instagram in 2012 for $1 billion when the company had no revenues and 13 employees. Many people thought it was a mistake. Now, the photo and video sharing platform exceeds billions of monthly users and is a key part of Facebook.[cccxlii]

Filter and Validate

I then apply a set of filters to my scenarios by asking a series of practical questions. Do they make sense? Applying proven laws like Metcalfe's Law, Moore's Law, and Cooper's Law, are they technically viable? What breakthroughs could disrupt the outcomes? What do "normal" people think?

The last question is perhaps most important because people are predictably unpredictable. We all have cultural, social, political, generational, and spiritual biases that impact what we accept and reject. Most people also need to see something to believe it is true, sometimes stopping promising innovation in its tracks. Finally, humans think linearly—A leads to B, B leads to C, and so on. In reality, technology is accelerating exponentially, and often one breakthrough annihilates a previous standard leading to entire new capabilities, so it's hard for us to imagine what the future looks like.

Predict, Learn, and Adjust

Once the filters have been applied to the scenarios, I develop my predictions. These typically take the form of short statements about what will happen in a given period of time. Importantly, I avoid using exact dates, because not even the best futurists really know for sure what the future holds.

I then vet my predictions in keynote presentations, thought leadership materials, and industry articles. I also update my predictions as new information and developments dictate. The process of predicting the future is really an ongoing virtuous cycle of gathering, vetting, validating, predicting, learning, and adjusting.

Companies are seeing the value of having prognosticators on their payroll as it helps to give them a competitive advantage. A quick search on the business-focused social network LinkedIn returns over 12,000 results when searching for futurists.

Even if you don't want to be a futurist, you can use these techniques to improve your life. After all, there's a little futurist in all of us.

ACKNOWLEDGMENT AND ATTRIBUTION

When looking for references or validation for some of my material, I often found myself returning to Wikipedia time and time again. This book uses significant references from Wikipedia which is released under the Creative Commons Attribution-Share-Alike License 3.0[cccxliii].

Wikipedia is a free online encyclopedia. It is created and edited by volunteers around the world. It is hosted by the Wikimedia Foundation. It is a free, high-quality resource. They survive by donations. If you use it frequently like I do, please consider donating. Any amount, even as small as a few dollars helps.

https://donate.wikimedia.org

I have no affiliation with the Wikimedia Foundation (the nonprofit organization that hosts Wikipedia).

Book cover design Sai P. via 99Designs.

https://99designs.com/

REFERENCES

[i] https://en.wikipedia.org/wiki/The_Jetsons

[ii] https://money.cnn.com/2017/01/02/technology/france-office-email-workers-law/index.html

[iii] https://www.oecd.org/sti/ieconomy/private-equity-investment-in-artificial-intelligence.pdf

[iv] https://www.statista.com/statistics/617136/digital-population-worldwide/

[v] http://www.itu.int/net/pressoffice/press_releases/2015/17.aspx#.VWS-F32Bjq-Q

[vi] http://www.esa.doc.gov/sites/default/files/emergingdig_0.pdf

[vii] https://www.statista.com/statistics/471264/iot-number-of-connected-devices-worldwide/

[viii] http://www.cs.ucsb.edu/~almeroth/classes/F04.176A/handouts/history.html

[ix] http://www.cs.ucsb.edu/~almeroth/classes/F04.176A/handouts/history.html

[x] https://en.wikipedia.org/wiki/DARPA

[xi] https://en.wikipedia.org/wiki/ARPANET

[xii] https://en.wikipedia.org/wiki/ARPANET

[xiii] https://www.thoughtco.com/ARPANET-the-worlds-first-internet-4072558

[xiv] https://en.wikipedia.org/wiki/Interface_Message_Processor

[xv] https://en.wikipedia.org/wiki/Node_(networking)

[xvi] https://www.computerworld.com/article/2593382/networking/networking-packet-switched-vs-circuit-switched-networks.html

[xvii] https://en.wikipedia.org/wiki/Telephone_switchboard

[xviii] https://www.computerworld.com/article/2593382/networking/networking-packet-switched-vs-circuit-switched-networks.html

[xix] https://en.wikipedia.org/wiki/IPv4

[xx] https://en.wikipedia.org/wiki/Routing_table

[xxi] https://en.wikipedia.org/wiki/Packet_switching

[xxii] https://searchnetworking.techtarget.com/definition/protocol
[xxiii] https://www.interserver.net/tips/kb/common-network-protocols-ports/
[xxiv] https://en.wikipedia.org/wiki/DECnet
[xxv] https://en.wikipedia.org/wiki/PDP-11_architecture
[xxvi] http://www.computinghistory.org.uk/det/3216/Digital-DECnet-Network-system/
[xxvii] https://en.wikipedia.org/wiki/Token_ring
[xxviii] https://en.wikipedia.org/wiki/AppleTalk
[xxix] https://en.wikipedia.org/wiki/Router_(computing)
[xxx] https://www.networkworld.com/article/2309917/lan-wan/lan-wan-router-man.html
[xxxi] https://en.wikipedia.org/wiki/Institute_of_Electrical_and_Electronics_Engineers
[xxxii] https://en.wikipedia.org/wiki/Internet_Protocol
[xxxiii] https://en.wikipedia.org/wiki/Vint_Cerf
[xxxiv] https://en.wikipedia.org/wiki/Bob_Kahn
[xxxv] https://en.wikipedia.org/wiki/Internet_Protocol
[xxxvi] https://en.wikipedia.org/wiki/OSI_model
[xxxvii] https://spectrum.ieee.org/tech-history/cyberspace/osi-the-internet-that-wasnt
[xxxviii] https://en.wikipedia.org/wiki/Internet_Protocol
[xxxix] https://en.wikipedia.org/wiki/Transistor
[xl] https://en.wikipedia.org/wiki/Transistor_count
[xli] https://en.wikipedia.org/wiki/Central_processing_unit
[xlii] https://en.wikipedia.org/wiki/Octet_(computing)
[xliii] https://support.microsoft.com/en-in/help/164015/understanding-tcp-ip-addressing-and-subnetting-basics
[xliv] https://en.wikipedia.org/wiki/IPv4
[xlv] https://en.wikipedia.org/wiki/Reserved_IP_addresses
[xlvi] https://en.wikipedia.org/wiki/Network_address_translation
[xlvii] https://en.wikipedia.org/wiki/IPv6
[xlviii] https://www.edn.com/electronics-blogs/other/4306822/IPV6-How-Many-IP-Addresses-Can-Dance-on-the-Head-of-a-Pin-
[xlix] https://www.internetsociety.org/resources/2018/state-of-ipv6-deployment-2018/
[l] https://internethalloffame.org/vint-cerf

[li] http://www.larryblakeley.com/requiem_for_%20ARPANET_vcerf.htm
[lii] https://en.wikipedia.org/wiki/Quantum_network
[liii] https://en.wikipedia.org/wiki/Cloud_computing
[liv] https://en.wikipedia.org/wiki/Plug-in
[lv] https://www.inc.com/tech-blog/interviewing-geoffrey-moore-core-versus-context.html
[lvi] https://en.wikipedia.org/wiki/Elasticity_(cloud_computing)
[lvii] https://en.wikipedia.org/wiki/Radio-frequency_identification
[lviii] http://www.dataversity.net/brief-history-internet-things/
[lix] https://iot-analytics.com/internet-of-things-definition/
[lx] https://www.cisco.com/c/dam/en_us/about/ac79/docs/innov/IoT_IBSG_0411FINAL.pdf
[lxi] https://www.the-ambient.com/guides/zigbee-vs-z-wave-298
[lxii] https://www.fiercecable.com/cable/comcast-quietly-buys-stringify-for-home-automation
[lxiii] https://ifttt.com/
[lxiv] https://support.apple.com/en-us/HT208940
[lxv] http://ioeassessment.cisco.com/
[lxvi] https://en.wikipedia.org/wiki/Social_network_analysis
[lxvii] https://en.wikipedia.org/wiki/Hacker
[lxviii] https://money.cnn.com/2016/10/21/technology/ddos-attack-popular-sites/index.html
[lxix] https://mysmahome.com/news/37402/15-iot-devices-use-default-passwords-research/
[lxx] https://money.cnn.com/2017/07/19/technology/fish-tank-hack-darktrace/index.html
[lxxi] https://securelist.com/ddos-report-in-q1-2018/85373/
[lxxii] https://en.wikipedia.org/wiki/Hacker
[lxxiii] https://en.wikipedia.org/wiki/Hacker
[lxxiv]
[lxxv] https://en.wikipedia.org/wiki/Internet_bot
[lxxvi] https://en.wikipedia.org/wiki/Internet_bot
[lxxvii] https://www.sciencenews.org/article/twitter-bots-fake-news-2016-election
[lxxviii] https://en.wikipedia.org/wiki/Botnet
[lxxix] https://www.symantec.com/connect/blogs/iot-devices-being-increasingly-used-ddos-attacks

THE INTERNET OF INTELLIGENT THINGS

[lxxx] https://www.networkworld.com/article/3123672/largest-ddos-attack-ever-delivered-by-botnet-of-hijacked-iot-devices.html

[lxxxi] https://www.businessinsider.de/hackers-stole-a-casinos-database-through-a-thermometer-in-the-lobby-fish-tank-2018-4?r=UK&IR=T

[lxxxii] https://www.ibtimes.co.uk/after-wannacry-experts-fear-worse-yet-come-more-cyberweapon-leaks-loom-1625086

[lxxxiii] https://www.incapsula.com/web-application-security/social-engineering-attack.html

[lxxxiv] http://teknologya.com/100-most-common-used-passwords-in-2017-are-you-using-one-of-them/

[lxxxv] http://teknologya.com/5-ways-create-secure-easy-remember-passwords/

[lxxxvi] https://mysmahome.com/news/37402/15-iot-devices-use-default-passwords-research/

[lxxxvii] https://mysmahome.com/news/37402/15-iot-devices-use-default-passwords-research/

[lxxxviii] https://quoteinvestigator.com/2017/07/16/product/

[lxxxix] https://www.theverge.com/2019/3/12/18259700/world-wide-wide-turns-30-www-anniversary-favorite-sites

[xc] https://en.wikipedia.org/wiki/Cryptocurrency

[xci] https://en.wikipedia.org/wiki/History_of_bitcoin

[xcii] https://www.coindesk.com/900-20000-bitcoins-historic-2017-price-run-revisited/

[xciii] https://en.wikipedia.org/wiki/Blockchain

[xciv] https://en.wikipedia.org/wiki/Linked_list

[xcv]

[xcvi]

[xcvii]

[xcviii] https://www.investing.com/crypto/currencies

[xcix] https://news.bitcoin.com/the-number-of-cryptocurrency-exchanges-has-exploded/

[c] https://coincentral.com/blockchain-hacks/

[ci] https://en.wikipedia.org/wiki/Secure_Hash_Algorithms

[cii] https://www.mycryptopedia.com/sha-256-related-bitcoin/

[ciii] https://www.consumerreports.org/privacy/consumers-had-email-and-passwords-exposed/

[civ] https://bitnodes.earn.com/?fref=gc

[cv] https://www.investopedia.com/terms/1/51-attack.asp

[cvi] https://www.coindesk.com/blockchains-feared-51-attack-now-becoming-regular

[cvii] https://blockgeeks.com/guides/blockchain-consensus/

[cviii] https://en.bitcoin.it/wiki/Proof_of_work

[cix] https://en.bitcoin.it/wiki/ASIC

[cx] https://www.cell.com/joule/fulltext/S2542-4351(18)30177-6

[cxi] https://www.blockchain-council.org/blockchain/what-are-the-alternative-strategies-for-proof-of-work/

[cxii] https://en.wikipedia.org/wiki/Proof-of-stake

[cxiii] https://en.wikipedia.org/wiki/Smart_contract

[cxiv] https://solidity.readthedocs.io/en/v0.5.3/

[cxv] https://blogs.cisco.com/digital/a-drop-of-water-begins-a-chain-reaction-infographic-tomorrowstartshere

[cxvi] https://venturebeat.com/2018/10/16/softbank-believes-1-trillion-connected-devices-will-create-11-trillion-in-value-by-2025/

[cxvii] https://spectrum.ieee.org/tech-talk/telecom/internet/popular-internet-of-things-forecast-of-50-billion-devices-by-2020-is-outdated

[cxviii] https://www.postscapes.com/internet-of-things-market-size/

[cxix] https://www.statista.com/statistics/471264/iot-number-of-connected-devices-worldwide/

[cxx] https://www.brainfacts.org/in-the-lab/meet-the-researcher/2018/how-many-neurons-are-in-the-brain-120418

[cxxi] https://phys.org/news/2018-06-ai-method-power-artificial-neural.html

[cxxii] https://www.seagate.com/files/www-content/our-story/trends/files/Seagate-WP-DataAge2025-March-2017.pdf

[cxxiii] https://www.ncbi.nlm.nih.gov/pmc/articles/PMC3068890/

[cxxiv] https://en.wikipedia.org/wiki/Industrial_Internet_of_Things

[cxxv] https://www.ge.com/digital/blog/everything-you-need-know-about-industrial-internet-things

[cxxvi] https://us.moocall.com/

[cxxvii] https://en.wikipedia.org/wiki/GSM

[cxxviii] https://www.cropx.com/

[cxxix] https://www.deere.com/en/technology-products/precision-ag-technology/

[cxxx] https://www.electronicdesign.com/analog/3-ways-iot-revolutionizes-farming

[cxxxi] https://agfundernews.com/what-is-precision-agriculture.html

[cxxxii] https://www.businessinsider.com/12-trillion-photos-to-be-taken-

in-2017-thanks-to-smartphones-chart-2017-8

[cxxxiii] https://mylio.com/true-stories/tech-today/heres-how-many-digital-photos-will-be-taken-in-2017-repost-oct

[cxxxiv] https://mylio.com/true-stories/tech-today/heres-how-many-digital-photos-will-be-taken-in-2017-repost-oct

[cxxxv] https://www.cisco.com/c/en/us/solutions/collateral/service-provider/visual-networking-index-vni/white-paper-c11-741490.html

[cxxxvi] http://highscalability.com/blog/2012/9/11/how-big-is-a-petabyte-exabyte-zettabyte-or-a-yottabyte.html

[cxxxvii] https://techcrunch.com/2010/08/04/schmidt-data/

[cxxxviii] https://www.forbes.com/sites/ciocentral/2012/04/24/the-web-is-much-bigger-and-smaller-than-you-think/#2e2c0ab47619

[cxxxix] https://www.forbes.com/sites/tomcoughlin/2018/11/27/175-zetta-bytes-by-2025/#82bbe8e54597

[cxl] https://www.seagate.com/files/www-content/our-story/trends/files/Seagate-WP-DataAge2025-March-2017.pdf

[cxli] https://en.wikipedia.org/wiki/Big_data

[cxlii] https://www.ericsson.com/assets/local/mobility-report/documents/2017/ericsson-mobility-report-june-2017.pdf

[cxliii] https://www.tubefilter.com/2019/05/07/number-hours-video-uploaded-to-youtube-per-minute/

[cxliv] https://www.forbes.com/sites/gilpress/2013/05/09/a-very-short-history-of-big-data/#5d3f8c6065a1

[cxlv] https://en.wikipedia.org/wiki/Nineteen_Eighty-Four

[cxlvi] https://www.amazon.com/1984-Classics-Go-George-Orwell-ebook/dp/B07JJ25HJC

[cxlvii] https://www.nsa.gov/about/mission-values/

[cxlviii] https://www.politico.com/story/2013/06/1984-book-sales-nsa-leak-092632

[cxlix] https://www.cctv.co.uk/how-many-cctv-cameras-are-there-in-london/

[cl] https://www.infographicsarchive.com/interesting-facts/infographic-much-data-nsa-look-daily/

[cli] https://freedomhouse.org/report/freedom-net/freedom-net-2018

[clii] https://www.theverge.com/2018/11/1/18050394/internet-freedom-report-2018-freedom-house-chertoff

[cliii] https://en.wikipedia.org/wiki/The_Conversation_(website)

[cliv] https://theconversation.com/chinas-social-credit-system-puts-its-people-under-pressure-to-be-model-citizens-89963

[clv] https://www.sciencealert.com/china-s-dystopian-social-credit-system-science-fiction-black-mirror-mass-surveillance-digital-dictatorship

[clvi] https://www.abc.net.au/news/2020-01-02/china-social-credit-system-operational-by-2020/11764740

[clvii] https://en.wikipedia.org/wiki/Sesame_Credit

[clviii] https://www.washingtontimes.com/news/2018/mar/16/china-touts-social-credit-system-to-deny-travel-on/

[clix] https://www.tsa.gov/news/releases/2018/10/15/tsa-releases-roadmap-expanding-biometrics-technology

[clx] https://www.independent.co.uk/news/uk/home-news/met-police-facial-recognition-success-south-wales-trial-home-office-false-positive-a8345036.html

[clxi] https://www.nytimes.com/2018/04/04/technology/mark-zuckerberg-testify-congress.html

[clxii] https://www.theverge.com/2019/7/24/20707013/ftc-facebook-settlement-data-cambridge-analytica-penalty-privacy-punishment-5-billion

[clxiii] www.eugdpr.org

[clxiv] https://ico.org.uk/for-organisations/guide-to-the-general-data-protection-regulation-gdpr/individual-rights/

[clxv] https://www.jdsupra.com/legalnews/public-agencies-and-gdpr-compliance-24422/

[clxvi] https://www.gdpreu.org/compliance/fines-and-penalties/

[clxvii] https://www.gdpreu.org/compliance/fines-and-penalties/

[clxviii] https://www.gdpreu.org/compliance/fines-and-penalties/

[clxix] https://www.theverge.com/2018/10/24/18017842/tim-cook-data-privacy-laws-us-speech-brussels

[clxx] https://www.digitaltrends.com/web/ways-to-decentralize-the-web/

[clxxi] https://solid.inrupt.com/

[clxxii] https://warwick.ac.uk/newsandevents/pressreleases/mass_proliferation_of/

[clxxiii] https://warwick.ac.uk/fac/sci/psych/people/thills/thills/2018_hillspopsdarksideofinfo.pdf

[clxxiv] https://warwick.ac.uk/newsandevents/pressreleases/mass_proliferation_of/

[clxxv] https://www.theguardian.com/technology/2019/feb/14/elon-musk-backed-ai-writes-convincing-news-fiction

[clxxvi] https://en.wikipedia.org/wiki/Mainstream_Science_on_Intelligence#CITEREFHauser2010

[clxxvii] https://en.wikipedia.org/wiki/Intelligence

[clxxviii] https://en.m.wikipedia.org/wiki/Intelligence

[clxxix] https://www.nytimes.com/1997/05/12/nyregion/swift-and-slashing-computer-topples-kasparov.html

[clxxx] https://en.wikipedia.org/wiki/AlphaGo_versus_Lee_Sedol

[clxxxi] https://en.wikipedia.org/wiki/Go_(game)

[clxxxii] https://www.quora.com/How-does-the-complexity-of-Go-compare-with-Chess

[clxxxiii] https://en.wikipedia.org/wiki/Reinforcement_learning

[clxxxiv] (https://deepmind.com

[clxxxv] https://en.wikipedia.org/wiki/Timeline_of_artificial_intelligence

[clxxxvi] https://en.wikipedia.org/wiki/History_of_artificial_intelligence

[clxxxvii] https://en.wikipedia.org/wiki/Arthur_Samuel

[clxxxviii] https://en.wikipedia.org/wiki/Supervised_learning

[clxxxix] https://en.wikipedia.org/wiki/Naive_Bayes_spam_filtering

[cxc] http://www.human-memory.net/brain_neurons.html

[cxci] http://www.enchantedlearning.com/subjects/anatomy/brain/Neuron.shtml

[cxcii] http://www.ascd.org/publications/books/199213/chapters/Losing-Your-Mind@-The-Function-of-Brain-Cells.aspx

[cxciii] https://en.wikipedia.org/wiki/User:Quasar_Jarosz. This file is licensed under the Creative Commons Attribution-Share Alike 3.0 Unported license. https://creativecommons.org/licenses/by-sa/3.0/deed.en

[cxciv] http://www.human-memory.net/brain_neurons.html

[cxcv] https://en.wikipedia.org/wiki/User:Quasar_Jarosz

[cxcvi] https://en.wikipedia.org/wiki/Neocortex

[cxcvii] https://en.wikipedia.org/wiki/Frank_Rosenblatt

[cxcviii] https://en.wikipedia.org/wiki/Feedforward_neural_network

[cxcix] https://en.wikipedia.org/wiki/Recurrent_neural_network

[cc] https://www.idc.com/getdoc.jsp?containerId=prUS44911419

[cci] https://teqmine.com/artificial-intelligence-business-risk/

[ccii] https://aiindex.org/

[cciii] https://www.independent.co.uk/life-style/gadgets-and-tech/news/facebook-artificial-intelligence-ai-chatbot-new-language-research-openai-google-a7869706.html

[cciv] https://www.facebook.com/dhruv.batra.dbatra?hc_ref=ARTU93AOPZc9m6qg01tRaPsce7X1wU5l-KJGVRmjCHEyKqiZZ-G86LS1xn3AxQSW31Hs

[ccv] https://languagelog.ldc.upenn.edu/nll/?p=33355

[ccvi] https://en.wikipedia.org/wiki/Michio_Kaku

[ccvii] https://www.outerplaces.com/science/item/17870-robots-need-inhibitor-chips-to-stop-them-from-slaughtering-all-of-mankind-claims-scientist

[ccviii] https://cs.stanford.edu/people/karpathy/deepimagesent/

[ccix] https://en.wikipedia.org/wiki/Recurrent_neural_network

[ccx] https://aiexperiments.withgoogle.com

[ccxi] https://photomath.net/

[ccxii] https://aiexperiments.withgoogle.com/autodraw

[ccxiii] http://bgr.com/2017/07/20/mit-food-recognition-app/

[ccxiv] https://www.theverge.com/2018/1/25/16931632/twitter-machine-learning-auto-image-cropping

[ccxv] https://www.excel-medical.com/solutions

[ccxvi] https://www.nbcnews.com/mach/science/doctors-have-trouble-diagnosing-alzheimer-s-ai-doesn-t-ncna815561

[ccxvii] https://www.connecterra.io/

[ccxviii] http://roboearth.ethz.ch/

[ccxix] https://en.wikipedia.org/wiki/Bernard_of_Chartres

[ccxx] https://en.wikipedia.org/wiki/Bernard_of_Chartres

[ccxxi] https://www.prnewswire.com/news-releases/parks-associates-more-than-one-in-four-us-broadband-households-own-a-smart-speaker-with-voice-assistant-300719144.html

[ccxxii] https://algorithmia.com/tags/machine-learning

[ccxxiii] https://www.raspberrypi.org/

[ccxxiv] https://en.wikipedia.org/wiki/Maker_culture

[ccxxv] https://aiyprojects.withgoogle.com/

[ccxxvi] https://techcrunch.com/2017/12/24/the-ai-chip-startup-explosion-is-already-here/

[ccxxvii] https://www.mouser.com/new/Intel/intel-movidius-stick/

[ccxxviii] https://en.wikipedia.org/wiki/Neuromorphic_engineering

[ccxxix] https://en.wikipedia.org/wiki/Neuromorphic_engineering

[ccxxx] https://futureoflife.org/autonomous-weapons-open-letter-2017/

[ccxxxi] https://qz.com/1616580/lethal-autonomous-weapons-could-become-a-reality-of-war/

[ccxxxii] https://www.vanityfair.com/news/2017/03/elon-musk-billion-dollar-crusade-to-stop-ai-space-x

[ccxxxiii] https://www.techworld.com/social-media/sir-tim-berners-lee-lays-out-nightmare-scenario-where-ai-runs-world-economy-3657280/

[ccxxxiv] https://www.bbc.com/news/technology-30290540

[ccxxxv] https://www.cnet.com/news/stephen-hawking-computers-will-overtake-humans-within-the-next-100-years/

[ccxxxvi] https://www.washingtonpost.com/news/innovations/wp/2015/03/16/googles-eric-schmidt-downplays-fears-over-artificial-intelligence/?utm_term=.4b7b3a5865ff

[ccxxxvii] http://www.bbc.com/news/31047780

[ccxxxviii] https://www.imdb.com/title/tt0086567/?ref_=nm_knf_t1

[ccxxxix] https://www.forbes.com/sites/blakemorgan/2018/09/05/robots-will-take-our-jobs-and-we-need-a-plan-4-scenarios-for-the-future/#3ce12e136db4

[ccxl] https://www.forbes.com/sites/quora/2018/01/18/technology-has-already-taken-over-90-of-the-jobs-humans-used-to-do/#a73b4e91bdd8

[ccxli] https://www.monster.com/career-advice/article/cool-future-jobs

[ccxlii] https://cacm.acm.org/news/244846-can-ai-become-conscious/fulltext

[ccxliii] https://cacm.acm.org/news/244846-can-ai-become-conscious/fulltext

[ccxliv] https://en.wikipedia.org/wiki/Neuromorphic_engineering

[ccxlv] https://en.wikipedia.org/wiki/Artificial_general_intelligence

[ccxlvi] https://en.wikipedia.org/wiki/Artificial_general_intelligence

[ccxlvii] https://www.technologyreview.com/2020/02/26/905777/google-ibm-quantum-supremacy-computing-feud/

[ccxlviii] https://thenextweb.com/artificial-intelligence/2018/02/06/heres-why-100-qubit-quantum-computers-could-change-everything/

[ccxlix] https://newatlas.com/physics/new-distance-record-quantum-entanglement-light-matter/

[ccl] https://www.sciencealert.com/scientists-just-unveiled-the-first-ever-photo-of-quantum-entanglement

[ccli] https://www.livescience.com/quantum-memory-entangled-far.html

[cclii] https://en.wikipedia.org/wiki/Absolute_zero

[ccliii] https://www.livescience.com/37807-brain-is-not-quantum-computer.html

[ccliv] https://www.kitp.ucsb.edu/mpaf

[cclv] https://phys.org/news/2018-03-quantum-international-collaboration-brain-potential.html

[cclvi] https://en.wikipedia.org/wiki/Quantified_self

[cclvii] https://www.smithsonianmag.com/history/tattoos-144038580

[cclviii] https://www.mc10inc.com/our-products

[cclix] https://www.wired.com/story/apple-watch-series-4/

[cclx] https://www.zdnet.com/article/how-apple-watch-saved-my-life/
[cclxi] https://www.sciencedirect.com/science/article/pii/S1388248113003640
[cclxii] https://stanfordhealthcare.org/health-care-professionals/medical-staff/medstaff-update/2014-october/stanford-implants-neurostimulator-intractable-epilepsy.html
[cclxiii] https://www.southampton.ac.uk/news/2009/10/communication-from-person-to-person-through-the-power-of-thought.page
[cclxiv] https://en.wikipedia.org/wiki/Locked-in_syndrome
[cclxv] http://ilabs.washington.edu/institute-faculty/bio/i-labs-andrea-stocco-phd
[cclxvi] https://www.nature.com/articles/s41598-019-41895-7
[cclxvii] https://www.technologyreview.com/s/612212/the-first-social-network-of-brains-lets-three-people-transmit-thoughts-to-each-others-heads/
[cclxviii] https://journals.plos.org/plosone/article?id=10.1371/journal.pone.0204566
[cclxix] https://singularityhub.com/2018/11/28/paralyzed-patients-can-now-control-android-tablets-with-their-minds
[cclxx] https://www.popsci.com/technology/article/2013-06/biohacking-implanted-headphones
[cclxxi] https://www.mercurynews.com/2013/12/20/computerizing-people-may-be-next-step-in-tech-2/
[cclxxii] http://www.dailymail.co.uk/sciencetech/article-2487100/Now-THATS-wearable-technology-Man-implants-mini-SKIN-track-body-temperature.html
[cclxxiii] https://www.ipsos.com/en-us/news-polls/more-americans-have-tattoos-today
[cclxxiv] https://www.technologyreview.com/s/611884/this-company-embeds-microchips-in-its-employees-and-they-love-it/
[cclxxv] https://www.independent.co.uk/voices/sweden-microchips-artificial-intelligence-contactless-credit-cards-citizen-science-biology-a8409676.html
[cclxxvi] http://www.sciencemag.org/news/2015/02/telescopic-contact-lenses-could-magnify-human-eyesight
[cclxxvii] https://www.sciencenews.org/article/new-artificial-eye-mimics-may-outperform-human-eyes
[cclxxviii] https://en.wikipedia.org/wiki/Transhumanism
[cclxxix] Buckminster Fuller's Knowledge Doubling Curve
[cclxxx] http://www.industrytap.com/knowledge-doubling-every-12-months-soon-to-be-every-12-hours/3950

[cclxxxi] https://www.npr.org/sections/thesalt/2016/07/15/485722228/where-did-agriculture-begin-oh-boy-its-complicated
[cclxxxii] https://en.wikipedia.org/wiki/555_timer_IC
[cclxxxiii] http://www.righto.com/2016/02/555-timer-teardown-inside-worlds-most.html
[cclxxxiv] https://en.wikipedia.org/wiki/Byte
[cclxxxv] https://en.wikipedia.org/wiki/Werner_Buchholz
[cclxxxvi] https://en.wikipedia.org/wiki/Byte
[cclxxxvii] https://en.wikipedia.org/wiki/Transistor_count
[cclxxxviii] https://www-03.ibm.com/press/us/en/pressrelease/52531.wss
[cclxxxix] https://en.wikipedia.org/wiki/Quantum_tunnelling
[ccxc] https://www.nanowerk.com/nanotechnology-news2/newsid=50895.php
[ccxci] https://www.technology.org/2020/05/11/new-recipe-for-single-atom-transistors-created-by-nist-scientists/
[ccxcii] https://en.wikipedia.org/wiki/Areal_density_(computer_storage)
[ccxciii] https://en.wikipedia.org/wiki/IBM_305_RAMAC
[ccxciv] https://www-03.ibm.com/ibm/history/exhibits/storage/storage_350.html
[ccxcv] https://www.themarysue.com/one-ton-harddrive/
[ccxcvi] http://www.computerhistory.org/storageengine/hdd-areal-density-reaches-1-terabit-sq-in/
[ccxcvii] https://actu.epfl.ch/news/storing-data-in-single-atom-magnets/
[ccxcviii] https://actu.epfl.ch/news/a-step-closer-to-single-atom-data-storage/
[ccxcix] https://en.wikipedia.org/wiki/Telnet
[ccc] https://fpcug.org/fb-downloadcalc.php
[ccci] http://www.businessinsider.com/5g-speed-network-lte-2017-3#what-is-5g-1
[cccii] https://help.netflix.com/en/node/306
[ccciii] https://www.digitaltrends.com/mobile/what-is-6g/
[ccciv] https://en.wikipedia.org/wiki/Last_mile
[cccv] https://en.wikipedia.org/wiki/Last_mile
[cccvi] https://en.wikipedia.org/wiki/IEEE_802.11ac
[cccvii] https://en.wikipedia.org/wiki/Martin_Cooper_(inventor)
[cccviii] https://en.wikipedia.org/wiki/Martin_Cooper_(inventor)
[cccix] https://en.wikipedia.org/wiki/MIMO
[cccx] https://www.sciencealert.com/researchers-have-achieved-wireless-speeds-of-1-tb-per-second

[cccxi] https://www.pcworld.com/article/242730/arm_cto_predicts_chips_the_size_of_blood_cells.html

[cccxii] https://en.wikipedia.org/wiki/ENIAC

[cccxiii] https://www.britannica.com/technology/ENIAC

[cccxiv] https://www.bls.gov/data/inflation_calculator.htm

[cccxv] http://www.microchip.com/about-us/company-information/about

[cccxvi] http://www.microchip.com/pdf/MCHP_to_Acquire_Atmel.pdf

[cccxvii] http://www.microchip.com/wwwproducts/en/ATtiny104

[cccxviii] The ATiny104 is even capable of faster speeds - "up to 12 MIPS Throughput at 12Mhz" according to the Atmel datasheet.

[cccxix] Adjusted for inflation. $5.5 million * 200

[cccxx] https://ourworldindata.org/coronavirus-data

[cccxxi] https://www.washingtonpost.com/news/capital-weather-gang/wp/2018/07/03/hot-planet-all-time-heat-records-have-been-set-all-over-the-world-in-last-week

[cccxxii] https://www.eurekalert.org/pub_releases/2018-05/ioap-ect052318.php

[cccxxiii] https://www.eurekalert.org/pub_releases/2018-05/ioap-ect052318.php

[cccxxiv] https://www.commondreams.org/news/2018/09/11/warning-existential-threat-humanity-un-chief-says-climate-change-moving-faster-we

[cccxxv] https://www.dw.com/en/world-hunger-on-the-rise-for-a-third-year/a-45440987

[cccxxvi] https://ourworldindata.org/life-expectancy

[cccxxvii] http://www.prb.org/Educators/TeachersGuides/HumanPopulation/Urbanization.aspx

[cccxxviii] http://www.unep.org/wed/quickfacts/

[cccxxix] https://www.theguardian.com/environment/2011/nov/28/un-farmers-produce-food-population

[cccxxx] https://www.theguardian.com/environment/2015/dec/02/arable-land-soil-food-security-shortage

[cccxxxi] https://www.zdnet.com/article/aging-water-infrastructure-wastes-17-trillion-gallons-a-year/

[cccxxxii] https://www.infrastructurereportcard.org/cat-item/drinking-water/

[cccxxxiii] https://www.businessinsider.com/mit-grad-made-a-robot-to-detect-water-pipe-leaks-2018-9

[cccxxxiv] https://www.sciencedaily.com/releases/2020/02/200220141748.htm

[cccxxxv] https://journals.ametsoc.org/doi/10.1175/WAF-D-18-0085.1?1=&

[cccxxxvi] https://foldingathome.org/2020/02/27/foldinghome-takes-up-the-fight-against-covid-19-2019-ncov/

[cccxxxvii] https://www.radiologybusiness.com/topics/artificial-intelligence/artificial-intelligence-ct-images-coronavirus-diagnosis

[cccxxxviii] https://www.medrxiv.org/content/10.1101/2020.02.27.20028027v2

[cccxxxix] https://www.usnews.com/news/best-countries/articles/2020-03-11/how-scientists-are-using-artificial-intelligence-to-track-the-coronavirus

[cccxl] https://www.iftf.org/

[cccxli] http://www.cnn.com/2015/05/14/tech/bioconcrete-delft-jonkers/

[cccxlii] https://techcrunch.com/2018/06/20/instagram-1-billion-users/

[cccxliii] https://creativecommons.org/licenses/by-sa/3.0

Made in the USA
Columbia, SC
05 December 2020